MW00808754

Temple of the Living Earth

The Story of the Awakening
of
A Priestess to the World

by Nicole Christine

Temple of the Living Earth cover artist: Sharon Nichols
Meditation on the art activates
the Temple of the Living Earth
thoughtform

Earth Song Publications

3400 E. Speedway Blvd. Suite 118-288
Tucson, Arizona 85716

© Copyright 1995 Nicole Christine

All Rights Reserved. Contact the publisher for written permission to reproduce any portions of this book.

Second Edition

Grateful acknowledgement is made to the following publishers and authors for permission to reprint quotations and/or include adaptions of their work:

"A Personal Message" by Chris Griscom, © cassette tape: The Light Institute, Galisteo, NM.

An Act of Faith by Jani King, © 1991; Triad Publishers, Cairns, Australia.

Earth Birth Changes by St. Germaine through Azena, © 1993; Triad Publishers, Cairns, Australia.

Gaia Matrix Oracle by Rowena Pattee Kryder, © 1991; Golden Point Productions, Mt. Shasta, CA.

God I Am by Peter Erbe, © 1993; Triad Publishers, Cairns, Australia.

SHE LIVES! The Return of the Great Mother by Judith Laura, © 1990; The Crossing Press, Freedom, CA.

The Star-Borne by Solara, © 1989; Star-borne Unltd. Charlottesville, VA.

Library of Congress Catalog Card Number: 95-061271

ISBN 0-9647306-0-X

Published by

Eᴀʀᴛʜ Sᴏɴɢ Pᴜʙʟɪᴄᴀᴛɪᴏɴѕ
3400 E. Speedway Blvd. Ste. 118-288
Tucson, Arizona 85716

Cover Art by Sharon Nichols
Graphics and typesetting by Michael Tyree

Printed with vegetable ink on acid-free paper by

MIϟϟION POϟϟIBLE
Commercial Printing

P.O. Box 1495
Sedona, AZ 86339

This book is dedicated to Divine Oneness
Individuated and Whole
In grateful acknowledgment
of
ALL THAT IS.

Dear Peggy –
Thank you for your gracious
sharing of your Temple home. I & five
Priestesses & 3 daughters, whose stories
branch out from this one, danced
in the 21 Praises to Tara.
Each of us have greatly benefitted
from your generousity.
Thank You! Thank You!
Nicole Christine
10/8/95

Temple Of The Living Earth

The Earth is a Living Spiritual Being in Her Own Right, with Her Own mind, consciousness, destiny and development. The Earth, Gaia, is a living organism within the Universal Living Organism. She is a Sacred Site. She is our Church, Temple, Sanctuary, Home, and Mother.

Guiding Principles Of
Earth/Gaian-Centered Spirituality

Honor Earth/Gaia as a Sacred Site and partake of her Fruit joyfully and gratefully. Honor the Life Force in ALL. Honor your body, hearth, and workplace as Temples of the Divine.

Live every moment as a Sacred Act in Alignment with Divine Source as you know and experience It.

Know Self as a unique, actualized, multidimensional, regenerative Being of unlimited creative and loving potential within the Cosmic Whole.

Live open-mindedly, thinking and feeling independently, for the Greatest Good. Unlearn false and outmoded teachings and conditionings. Gratefully exercise the gift of the right of free will, responsibly and honestly.

Live in Freedom by breaking through form into formless form, into Spirit and Wholeness.

Know the Silence and merge with It. Honor the creative power of the Word. Avoid unnecessary, unclear verbiage and waste of the priceless Breath of Life.

Live and speak the Highest Truth, as you know it, moment-to-moment, for the Highest Good. Honor and encourage the Highest Truth of others in the darkness and the light.

Stimulate inner awareness and multisensory perceptions to heighten communication with ALL LIFE and enhance Cosmic consciousness. Commune with Father Sky and Mother Earth as directly and respectfully as a Loving Child communes with Loving Parents.

Commit to the Sacred Marriage through inner union of the Divine Feminine and Divine Masculine, of feeling and thought.

Live responsibly in co-creative, co-operative partnership with the Earth, Nature and One Another.

Live in Balance, Beauty, Love, Harmony and Good Humor.

Live attentively. Trust, attune and respond to the synchronistic Life Process.

Live in the natural flow of Abundance, Simplicity and All Good Things. Give and receive generously.

*LIVE LIFE FULLY AND GRATEFULLY!
CELEBRATE CREATION!*

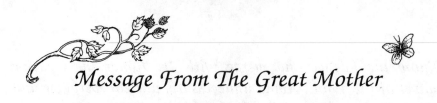

Message From The Great Mother

In January of 1991, a group of women gathered for a California mountain Women's Writing Retreat. When it was time to go back into the World where Middle-Eastern oil fields were burning and the rivers and the gulf were poisoned, we contemplated what was coming. In prayer, I asked Our Great Mother what was ahead and entered Her response in my journal. I include Her Words here for Peace and Posterity.

That which is coming is the ability to

LIVE

THE BEST of Possible Lives

In the worst of times . . .

Beloved Daughter . . . you have stumbled and fallen

but you have never given up

Your Time is NOW

for where there was hate, you chose Love

where there was war, you chose Peace

where there was doubt, you chose Hope

where there was separation, you chose Wholeness

And now in the worst of times, you are choosing, you are committed, to Walk The Beauty Way. You are not alone. Join hands with your sisters. Join hands with your brothers. Walk on with Beauty around you, Beauty above you, Beauty before you, Beauty behind you, Beauty below you. You are Beauty Within and Without. And you know that more deeply for Keeping the Lodge with your sisters who have filled your soul with Beauty. For Beauty is what they are. That is what you are. In Beauty there is Truth. In Truth there is always a Better Way . . . the Best of All Possible Ways in the Worst of Times . . . the Best, which is less than a step away.

Contents

In The Beginning

The telling of this story began as a doctoral dissertation submitted to and honored by the International Fellowship of Isis, Clonegal Castle, Ireland. It was entitled The Temple of Gaia and Green Man. It is not an academic treatise. The story takes you into the inner chambers of my consciousness and is written in the style of the subjective feminine. It is a living, evolving tale of the return of the Goddess and Her Priestesses and Priests. It is a journey into wholeness and balance for women and men because the Creatrix shares Creation with the Creator.

Part One is an expanded version of the dissertation written early in 1992. It is an Earth-Honoring Matrix for the 1990's that I spun and wove as a Crystal Priestess of Gaia. Part Two is a sharing of the early stages of this Sacred Work through February 2, 1995. It contains the Beauty, Mystery and Magic of living contemporary life as a Priestess to the World.

The overall content of this work is true according to the bias of my personality and my degree of consciousness. Persons included in this writing, who are related to as public figures, are referred to by their actual names. Fictionalized names and, sometimes, places have been used to protect the privacy of other individuals. There is a myriad of children, women and men who have touched my life, and thus this story, whom I cannot mention by any name. They are forever imprinted in my heart.

Given that my writing approach is conversational rather than literary, I have taken liberties with the formal written word and honored the flow of my consciousness. At times, this work takes on the flavor of a personalized curriculum guide, other times more the flavor of a discovery process, testimony, or her-story. At all times, I hope it inspires you to live your story more fully. The content may further activate your own awakening. Therefore, you may find it beneficial to create sacred space for yourself whenever you read it.

I introduce books that have influenced my journey in much the same way I introduce people. I thank all the authors and publishers who gave me permission to reprint quotations from their works or to include adaptions of their material. And I thank each individual who helped me edit and proof this book.

Gender inclusive language is used throughout this book. In cases where the reading flow would be disrupted by using he and she, Priest and Priestess, God and Goddess, the feminine form is used. She is not present in he, but he is present in **she**, Priest is in **Priest**ess, God is in **God**dess.

Nicole Christine, D.D. (Daughter of Divinity)

Part One

The Temple

*T*his is the time of reawakening. It is the time of remembering that the Earth is our Temple. Time to remember that the very ground we walk upon is the temple floor and that the sky above is the temple roof. It is the time to tear down inner and outer walls that create the illusion that our spiritual and material natures are separate, oppositional realities. Time to live the fullness and exhilaration of our Earthwalk in co-creative oneness with All That Is.

It is time to acknowledge that each of us is Priest and Priestess, unto ourselves, in ever refining attunement and collaboration with Creation. There is no outside mediator between Heaven and Earth that can possibly intervene on our behalf or interpret Truth that we somehow cannot access. Heaven and Earth are one, and we are one with Heaven and Earth.

In this dimension of Creation called Earth, we are being called upon to walk openly, in great humility and joy, as Priests and Priestesses to the World. The Great Mother is gently awakening us to the reality that Her Daughter Gaia is a single living organism with Her own divine cosmic destiny; a destiny in which we each play intricate and essential parts. The Great Father is urging us to open our eyes and see His part in Creation through the eyes of His son Green Man, who knows and utters the secrets of Nature. This ancient archetype, signifying irrepressible life, is reappearing to counterbalance our outrageous disregard for nature and life itself.

In our sleep, we had many dreams of what we are not. It is now time to rise up and live the awakened dream of our True Reality as Gaian Priestesses and Green Man Priests. We can do this simply by breathing in this cosmic consciousness and allowing it to fill our being. Thus it can move through us in a constant recycling process of pure Creative Essence that naturally activates our God/Goddess Realized Potential.

While asleep, we imagined the material realm as the only plane of existence and created illusions of duality and separation. We conjured up painful misperceptions that seemed to split our very souls, our very brains, in half. We imagined a division between our masculine and feminine aspects. Thus we created an effect of separation of the right and left hemispheres of our brains, of our hearts and minds, of feelings and thoughts, of inner and outer realities, of spirit and matter. We believed that matter is inert, somehow separate from spirit that permeates all that is. In this deluded state of consciousness, we separated ourselves from one another, and from nature.

In the early dawn of this new day, we can be of great service to ourselves and the planet as Gaian Priestesses and Green Man Priests. Each Gaian Priestess mirrors the feminine qualities of the Earth Mother and inspires others of her gender. She also mirrors the inner female for men. Green Man Priests bring forth the qualities of nature in man and of the masculine aspects in the World. They serve as an evolved reflection for other males and the inner male of women.

Encoded within the genetic makeup of each of us is the Divine Design of our True Nature in right relationship to our planet and All Our Relations. The Priestess in each of us knows how to break the code. She has the power to move us out of old limiting practices into full, free expression of our authentic selves. With discernment, the Priestess harvests the fruits of the past that nurture us as we build anew. Simultaneously, she allows fruit that no longer nourishes to decay and enrich the soil of the New Earth. She has the power to lift the veil of illusion so that the mysteries are no longer hidden behind temple walls, underground in kivas, or within cloistered minds. She wants us to abandon old habits of believing we are separate from Source; and that others, more powerful and outside of us, can show us the way. The Truth, the Great Mystery, is fully accessible to all who ask with pure intention. Ask and the code is broken. Ask and the veil is lifted. Ask and the walls tumble down. Ask and the inner fuses with the outer. Ask and the Priestess within will reveal the Truth of All That Is and guide you in living that Truth.

What is revealed will reverberate with the timeless force and wisdom of the Ancient Ones. It will be cradled by the matriarchal hands and heart of the Goddess, influenced by patriarchal religions and ascended master teachings, and garbed in new age visions. Most certainly, the revelation will be grounded in the indigenous ways of unity with, and reverence for, All Our Relations. However, the time, shape, way and form of each individual's revelation will be precisely pertinent to him or her. As our individual awareness heightens, and we attune to our own process and modality, we will consciously experience the unfoldment of our shared journey and the story of the One expressing as the Many.

The Priestess that I am, within and without, is spinning and weaving this matrix. She is utilizing symbolism and forms relevant to me, as a way of breaking my code so that I may know myself and all others as fully actualized, multi-dimensional, God/Goddess Realized Beings. As such, we are aligning with this inevitable, collective process of rediscovering how to live in harmony with nature and one another. This matrix, committed to form by the written word, casts a mold in human consciousness. This matrix, committed to form by action, becomes my work in the Awakened Reality, the New Earth Culture. Inspired by the *Gaia Matrix Oracle,* as I spin and weave, I hold this as my personal purified intention:

I, Nicole Christine, in the ancient tradition as a High Priestess of the Great Mother and in my new World perceptions as a Crystal Priestess of Gaia, make this commitment:

- *to consistently practice spiritual ecology,*

- *to actively participate in and contribute to the transformation from localized Earth-abusive, ecocidal culture to globalized Earth-Honoring, co-creative culture,*

- *to be vitally aware of the sacredness of All Life,*

- *to joyfully facilitate the healing of the Earth by healing myself, and*

- *to diligently move from mutual reactiveness, helplessness and blame to responsiveness, co-creativity and harmony.*[1]

To this new matrix, process, and purpose, I dedicate all my time, energies, talents and resources. To this commission, I pledge to consciously and wholeheartedly hold the Immaculate Concept of the Divine Thoughtform that each human being on the planet is a Priest and Priestess to the World.

It is done and it is so in the Sacred Names of Gaia and Green Man.

My Scriptures . . .
Our Scriptures

Scriptures are any sacred writings. When I accept the sacredness of my life, of all life, my story becomes scripture and the telling of it becomes a sacred act. My life, my story, interweaves with the life and story of every other human being and every other aspect of Creation. And so Our Story is sacred. Our Story is Scripture.

There is no beginning, there is no end, to our story. Thus to tell it, I may pull out any page from our scripture as a starting point. I could start lifetimes ago when I was a temple scribe, but I choose instead to simply bring forth that consciousness to further the work of recording this piece. I have picked a date, a moment, not too long ago in this lifetime. Dates, times and places give us parameters for human experience. They are helpful reference points for telling our stories. They assist me in telling the story of my inner journey merging with my outer one and of my scriptures merging into our scriptures and our new reality.

On October 5, 1990, I, nearly half a century in age, rededicated the rest of this life to the Goddess. I say rededicated because once we were all dedicated to Her. She went through a regenesis in the fertile darkness of the underworld and is now ascending. Her ascent is expedited in proportion to our willingness, as women and men, to bring forth anew the feminine qualities of allowance and acceptance, of beauty and wisdom.

A month earlier, I had departed from family, friends and my northern

California home. All I owned was in my van that was now my home. For the first hour of my journey, I grieved about what I was leaving behind and what had never been while I was there. Suddenly, my tears ceased as the freedom of the open road activated my sense of adventure. I was embarking on a spiritual pilgrimage that would end on October 6, 1991. That date would be the sixth year anniversary of a mystical experience that greatly expanded my consciousness. I shifted emotional gears and eagerly sped ahead!

The Goddess was my guide. My first stop was at Ananda Village in Nevada City just four hours south of what had been my home. For three weeks, I camped under tall healing pines and found comfort in the nurturing Presence of the Divine Mother. I spent the next two weeks exploring the back country of Nevada, Utah, and Colorado, absorbing the beauty of the Earth Mother. How renewing it was to be embraced in the many arms of the Goddess.

On the fifth day of October in the year nineteen and ninety, she led me to Bandelier National Park in northern New Mexico where Pueblo Ancestors reside on the other side of the camp. It was time for the Daughter to return to the Mother, for ego-self to bow to the Goddess Within. Time to dedicate the rest of my life to serving the Great Mother in my own right, true to the individuated aspect of her that I was created to express.

At Bandelier, I was inwardly guided to trek three miles down Frijoles Canyon to the muddy Rio Grande River. I weighed myself down unnecessarily with a bulky sweater and a heavy notebook crammed into my backpack with ritual objects, nuts and water. I was wearing well-worn jeans and a light sweat shirt. My journey began at 6,000 feet along a vibrant stream adorned by green and gold vegetation. The descent to the Upper Waterfall and then to the Lower Waterfall was pleasant. Beyond the lower falls the terrain startlingly changed.

An ominous fence line appeared, symbolizing my crossover point into the underworld. Fear gripped me as I perceived desert harshness, snake country. I trekked through surrealistically burned, parched, wind and flood worn land. Several times I wanted to turn back, but knew I could not. This, too, was the World of the Mother, as barren and desolate as the land my soul had traveled through in recent years.

Finally, I reached the Rio Grande. I wandered down-river until I spotted my ritual site. I stopped a few yards away from the pubic Venus mound of dirt covered with green hair. Here I honored the muddy menses flowing downstream. Raising my arms in Priestess pose, I asked the Great Mother, the Spirits of This Place, the Four Elements, and the Four Directions for permission to be there and to perform my rite. Permission was granted. Where debris had collected by the mound, I dug a small hole in the mud and sprinkled sage and grain in it. I added two tubes of lipstick, a razor and mascara. These were patriarchal artifacts I had used to pay supreme tribute to false images and artificiality. I thanked them for their lessons as

I buried them over with mud. I sprinkled more sage and grain on top, then packed the ground with my moccasined feet.

Next, I took out a green malachite egg given me by a sister who knows death well. Then a vision quest figurine made by a sister who daily struggles to integrate the worlds of her red and her white lineages. I held them in the water as a blessing, then reverently placed them on the mound, adding sage, three almonds, a feather, a lamb bone, and grain. A nearby plant gave-away three clusters of three buds for my two sisters and me. In thanksgiving to the Spirits of Place, the Four Elements, and the Four Directions, I tossed grain in each direction. It was done. I had returned to the Mother. Wholeness was ensured and I gave thanks.

The ascent was harder than the descent, but I was more accepting of that. I was more gentle with myself than I have been in other slow ascents. I climbed. I rested. I climbed some more. At the top, I nourished myself with squash salad I had prepared that morning. Gratefully, ingesting this gift of the Earth Mother, I felt at peace. A deep sense of rightness permeated my being as I headed my van toward Santa Fe. It was good to feel alive again.

ॐ

I explored the Santa Fe area for two weeks. Then I moved on to the Light Institute in Galisteo to continue inner work I began there in the autumn of 1988. I had, through past life exploration and clearing, more fully aligned with my Higher Self and connected with my inner child in all her innocence and woundedness. During the intervening two years, this child had taken me deep into the depths of cultural dysfunctionalism that permeates family systems. By reconnecting with that despair, she and I learned to heal and to reclaim our divinity. She, whose name by birth is Linda Lou, was persistently reminding me how to play. She was quasi-successful.

After completing the first session series in 1988, I received a cassette tape recorded by Light Institute founder and director, Chris Griscom. It was a personal message for those who completed work there. Her opening remarks made a deep imprint in my consciousness.

"All of you who have found your way here to the Light Institute are friends. Are known to us who are known to you. You created us to be those who open the door, who are the ones standing at the threshold for you so that you could move through that threshold with the Guidance of your Higher Self. That Higher Self that each one of you has carried from your conception in this lifetime, brought you to the Light Institute in order for you to awaken to your true path of divinity and manifestation within this chosen lifetime. You come here in order to uncover, to unfold, your True Self and to allow that Self to become visible to the world around you because you have the courage to be who you truly are; and you chose this lifetime to manifest a blueprint already divinely designed by you. Each one of you had profound experiences of self-recognition and self-exploration here at the

11

Light Institute, and the energy that was released and created and stimulated here is echoing out from you now."[2]

I did not feel very courageous about being who I truly am. My tendency was to entrap myself in a situation, most often in a male/female love relationship. Therein, I let my true self and the true self of my partner become so diminished that I would virtually start to die. This pattern was scary and baffling because my involvements were with good men, often exceptionally good men. I often stayed until I had little more than enough life force to get out the door. Once out, I would desperately seek myself anew. Having just left my fourth marriage, I was indeed "standing at the threshold." I clearly needed help in moving through it.

Being at the Light Institute is like being in a time warp. The old Spanish adobe village of Galisteo floats in unformed openness of land and sky, jarring one out of singular dimensional stuckness. The energies of the Light Institute, the personnel and Higher Self collaborate to do the rest of what it takes to move one into multi-dimensional awareness.

The inner work series I was now undertaking focused on past lives with my parents. I was here to heal and truly comprehend the impact we had on one another lifetime after lifetime. I realized that my dedication ritual to the Great Mother prepared me for this work because the newborn child looks to his or her Earth parents as God and Goddess. Neither the child nor the parents are ever free to be their True Selves unless these relationships are realigned into true cosmic perspective. During the sessions, I moved in consciousness through lifetimes when I had been a parent, a sibling, a mate, an enemy, a Priest, or a follower to my father, my deceased biological mother or my stepmother. I was able to release us all to the More, freed from the narrow mental and emotional constructs of how we related in this one lifetime. I even felt releases in the relationships with my two grown sons. I felt able to embrace life cycles, to more freely dance the spiral dance of Creation.

By the end of my week in Galisteo, an enormous amount of revitalized energy was charging through me as I again set out in my van that I call the White Buffalo. "What next?" I asked driving away from my adobe way station and back into time.

"Tucson," the Goddess whispered.

ॐ

I meandered a bit and camped near the Verde River south of Sedona, Arizona. I even challenged the guidance to go to Tucson when I found a riverside house available to rent, but all my efforts to bring that about bizarrely fell through. Clearly, this was not where the Goddess wanted me to be. Nights were getting colder, making sleeping in my van less enjoyable. On the cool morning of October 21, I headed south for Tucson. At nightfall, I snuggled under covers in a cozy studio apartment bed for what I deemed to be the first night of a temporary stay.

On the fourth day, vivid clues led me to what was on the other side of the threshold crossed in Galisteo. The Goddess guided me to a temple and college I did not know existed and to those who were on the other side of the door waiting to assist me. Lady Elena and Lord Kenneth, ordained Priestess and Priest Hierophants in the International Fellowship of Isis, met with me that day. Within two hours, I enrolled in a Priestess training program scheduled to begin early in November and end at the Summer Solstice in June with an ordination ceremony.

I felt deep mystical wonderment and a "but, of course" reaction to the path opening before me. Despite patriarchy's overt and covert attempts to destroy the Goddess for thousands of years, she was alive and well in Tucson, Arizona in 1990! And she had guided me to Her sanctuary even though I had only vague recollection (from where, I knew not) that many call her Isis. I had not heard of the Ireland-based Fellowship of Isis or its Sacred Work that was spreading around the World.

Founders Lawrence, Pamela, and Olivia Durdin-Robertson established the external organization in 1976. This hereditary Priestly line comes to them from the Egyptian Princess, Scota, a Daughter of Isis. The Fellowship manifesto concludes with these words: *Priestesses, Priests, every member, have equal honor. Every human, animal, bird, and tree are an eternal offspring of the Mother Goddess' Divine Family of Life.* After a lifetime of wandering, both my inner child and the reawakening Priestess within had found a home where the Mother/Father God resided in harmony. A harmony that would gradually manifest for me and for all, everywhere.

之

During the 12-day interim period between the time I enrolled in the Priestess program and the first class, I had time to become reacquainted with Tucson. I lived in this verdant Sonoran Desert oasis during the early seventies when it was much smaller. There was still a small town feel in the older areas now preserved as historical districts. The patio of my favorite Fourth Avenue restaurant, La Indita, looked colorfully the same, and the spicy food tasted as good as I remembered it to be. I was excited about people-centered changes in Tucson life: the Downtown Saturday Night street scene and the now annual October Chili Festival held at the Botanical Gardens. Bigger changes —widespread crimes against nature and humanity — disturbed me. Sprawling growth uprooted the giant Saguaros and paved over the pathways of the coyote and javalina. Wrought iron window bars imprisoned people and their fears in stores and homes throughout every part of town.

But I spent most of my time reflecting on my spiritual journey. What I sometimes viewed as erratic experiences now synchronistically fit together. The most pivotal occurrences began in the mid-eighties while I was living and teaching in an inner city community in the greater Los Angeles area. When my sons, my second husband and I moved there nearly a decade earlier, my sons adamantly professed their intent to stay put until they finished high school. "Mom, you may be a gypsy, but we're not," they declared. "We don't want to keep changing schools and leaving friends."

And stay we did, though I divorced and remarried and divorced again during that time. I also advanced my education to a master's degree level, earned a teaching credential, and became a highly regarded adult educator. My oldest son, Joel, graduated from high school and moved out on his own. By the time Todd, my youngest son, reached his senior year, I was feeling impatient to leave the megalopolis. Impatient to live a more spiritually centered life. In the early 1980s, I followed the path of Self-Realization and determined that Paramahansa Yogananda was a Masterful Guide on my path, but not my guru. I was gratefully influenced by his teachings, particularly those that spoke of the Divine Mother who "is closer than the Father."

During this period, I became conscious of the Invisible Ones. Eastern meditation practices did not fit into my action-filled life. I was a single working mom earning a Master's Degree and, somehow, fitting in a good deal of time in grassroots community efforts to develop multi-cultural education in my sons' school district. I got up at dawn and seldom went to bed before midnight. I did not believe that sitting in meditation was the only way to connect with the Divine and decided to develop communion in the same ways I developed it in the physical realm. I love to write letters, so I wrote letters to the Divine Mother. When taking breaks from my work, I invited Babaji or Buddha to walk with me. When dancing, I took Krishna as a partner. When needing a shoulder to lean on, I turned to Jesus whom I had come to know as Sananda. Always, they were only a thought away. By simply turning my consciousness to them as I would a friend, they were present and responsive. Their Presence, Love, and Guidance were always available to me in interactive ways because I did not need them to use precious life force energy to materialize as proof of their existence.

I acquired a more palpable perspective of Jesus, the Christ as one of the Masters in the Self-Realization lineage of gurus. Here he was not the crucified martyr forever hanging on the cross. He was revered as an evolved Being of embodied Christ Consciousness with the message that we could and would do that which he had done on Earth and more.

More recently, I had connected with a community of students of A Course In Miracles. Through these studies, I healed more inculturated misconceptions of this Elder Brother and came to see his life, his mission, from a broader perspective. The freer I became of old attitudes toward him, the more I felt his presence. I countered my frustrations with urban life by daydreaming of the possibility of moving to the mountains in a year to help develop an evolving Course In Miracles retreat center. There I imagined myself living in peaceful serenity and constant communication with the Divine.

But I was in my neighborhood Laundromat, when I consciously received my first message from him in September of 1984. The place was nosier than usual. A baby crying. Youngsters running. Two ghetto blasters blasting raucous music on different stations. *One more year*, I thought loudly to myself as I furiously folded clothes so I could leave. *One more year and I can leave the city!*

The telepathic message, unmistakably, from Sananda/Jesus, the Christ, pressed through so strongly and clearly that I stopped working. I pulled out sheets of brown paper toweling from a nearby dispenser and wrote down his words. *Dear One, you have unfinished work as a teacher and a mother. Do not approach the year ahead with an attitude of filling time. The only moment is NOW. And I Am in all places, people and things. When your present work nears completion, you will be redirected. Do not become preoccupied with when or how this will be. Just know that it will be.*

I felt enveloped in absolute stillness even though the surrounding commotion continued. His words catapulted me into a deeper sense of destiny. *You will come to understand how the work you are doing now and the bonds you are making will link up to your future. You already sense that your diverse life experiences have been preparation for what is to be. Your yearning for the land and a simple, uncluttered way of living will ease as you accept that your heart's desire is being fulfilled.*

His next words triggered a soft sob followed by tears. *Continue to love your sons in all things for they were your first teachers of unconditional love. You allowed yourself to feel burdened with responsibilities. First, as the eldest child and only sister to your younger brothers. Then, as a single mother of two sons. You know now that I AM your Elder Brother and have always been with you. Take my hand. Your step is getting lighter as you walk with me and your newly found spiritual family into the Light of God's Eternal Love.*

His hand was always there for me in the year ahead —when I remembered to reach out for it. And when the time came, I was clearly guided. The house sold the very day it went on the market. Escrow closed the week after I completed my teaching contract and Todd's senior year ended. He moved into an apartment with a friend. The retreat center had become a reality and I could live there in a donated camping trailer. I could leave the city and climb the mountain. I was going home.

Come, my child. Come Home. Come Home. A wondrously gentle Voice called to me in my sleep . . . called with love and tenderness far surpassing the call of the most caring Earthly parent awakening a beloved child. I lay serenely still without opening my eyes. The absorbing, ethereal Voice called again. *Come Home, my child. Your time is now.* The Call was but a whisper . . . a whisper so mighty no other sound dare intrude.

Slowly, I opened my eyes. It was still dark outside, but a soft glowing light filled the trailer. Though I had spent many days and nights camping at the retreat center, the familiar was now surreal. I touched my face to be sure I was physically present and felt tears trickling down my cheeks. Images of my two sons filled my mind and tears flowed freely. Tears of gratitude.

Of love. Of joy. Of hope for their own awakenings. I recalled that midsummer I became aware I would be going Home soon and had asked that it not be before Todd's eighteenth birthday. He turned eighteen on October 1, 1985. It was now early morning on October 6. I had been given the asked for extension. My time was now.

Come. Come, my child. The Voice was still calling with indescribable love and patience. I reached for my pale pink robe and slipped into it. The radiance filling the trailer brightened as I rose and stepped into my slippers. Mesmerized, I took the few steps to the trailer door. I opened it and studied the night before me. Nearby, Live Oak trees were illumined by the moon playing behind small puffy clouds. Familiar sounds of night creatures greeted me. I stepped onto the land I so loved. Its surface, still dusty from Indian Summer heat and dryness, had a golden filigree look. I felt powerfully drawn to the Voice seeming to originate from the road many yards away. Lightly, I began walking along the dirt driveway. Going Home . . . Going Home . . . Going Home . . .

I moved with infinitesimal ease and grace. Closer. Closer to Home. The Voice was getting fainter. The Stillness stronger. Peace more powerful. Joy more encompassing. The Earth dissolving more with each step I took. I felt as if I was walking out of my body. I wondered if it, too, was dissolving or if it would be found in the morning on the road like a towel dropped on the floor after a shower. I was ascending on an invisible path into Healing White Light, into God's Presence. We were walking together. I stopped and surrendered fully into the Light. Into Oneness. Suddenly, nothing existed but Love. Pure, Pure Love. Only LOVE. Vibrant and encompassing LOVE.

I was Home! I had found my way back to our Father! Never had I felt so secure and so willing to be cared for. Nothing exists but Love as a constant. I did not get or give it. IT IS LOVE. LOVE IS IT. I AM LOVE. LOVE IS I. YOU ARE LOVE. LOVE IS YOU. GOD IS LOVE. LOVE IS GOD. LOVE, ONLY LOVE.

A knowing filled me. A knowing of our Oneness with the Father, with one another, with ALL THAT IS. A knowing of our Immortality, our Innocence, our Goodness, our Beauty.

And from this state of knowing, I understood I had left "loose-ends." Through thought, I acknowledged that I did not want to leave the litter of my unfinished business on the planet. In the instant of that acknowledgment, I found myself again in my body with my feet on the ground. But I did not feel like a body. I did not feel a part of this World. I was Light and Love and everything about me was less dense, more translucent.

I returned to the trailer, gliding, more than walking. I looked inside. It was still aglow. I sat in the open doorway looking out into the iridescent night sky. The clouds had the same silvery radiance as the moon. They beamed instructions to me regarding what I needed to do to tie up my loose-ends. Further guidance was to stay open to new information. For now, I was to return to bed for a few more hours sleep before the coming dawn.

I felt wonderfully safe and loved as I snuggled back into my sleeping bag. As I closed my eyes, I knew I would never again forget my origin — who I AM, who we are — no matter how much longer I stayed on this plane of existence.

ə

In the weeks and months ahead, I realized Home was a state of be-ingness rather than a place. More importantly, I grasped that my awakening experience somehow turned my attention away from the Father's outer do-main to the inner hearth of the Mother. In choosing to return Home to the Father, I began receiving the tender loving care of The Blessed Mother. And the more I focused inwardly on Her Presence, the more visible she became in my outer reality.

Her boldest appearance came to me via the book, *Blessed Among Women*. I resonated with the absorbing portrayal of her life as told by Arnold Michael and I wrote him to express my deep gratitude for his work. A short time later, I received a surprising invitation to visit him and his wife, Kay.

The invitation had the same serene summoning quality I felt when the Voice called me Home that October night. Mid-July of the next year, I made the five-hour drive to meet the Michaels. I felt honored and a bit mystified because the note indicated that they rarely had guests because Arnold's health was failing. They received me cordially. Reverend Michael shared his vision of the Madonna Ministry that he had founded under the guidance of Mother Mary. Its ministers helped bring forth the divine feminine re-emerg-ing on this planet. An hour into the visit, he abruptly asked, "Do you feel called to be ordained in the Ministry?"

My response was firm, flat. "No."

"Think it over," he said gently. "Now I need rest."

He retired to nap and I walked about the house convinced there was nothing to think over. Called? I simply was not minister material.

I would like you to say "yes," my child.

I quickly turned in the direction of the Voice. My eyes fixated on a stunningly beautiful painting of Mary. Her Presence filled the room, instantly dissolving my resistance. I responded with unequivocal certainty. "Yes, Mother. Yes."

I felt her smile. She knew my answer to her Call before I did. Telepathi-cally, I understood the ordination as an initiation rather than a ministry. It outwardly symbolized my inward dedication to the Sacred Feminine energies and indicated readiness to accept an intensified degree of Inner Realm de-velopment. As I acknowledged my readiness, I again experienced ALL THAT IS as LOVE, ONLY LOVE.

And so it came to pass, in the Year of Our Lady, 1986. I became an Initiate of Mary. I now knew the Mother and the Father as One. I awakened to the knowing that we are all Home in that Oneness, in that LOVE.

ə

The Goddess had always been with me revealing one of her many faces whenever I needed her. Always there. Holding everything together. In the background, hardly visible, like women everywhere. My own yearning to be visible matched the intensity of my desire for her to be visible in my daily life. I sought her out as Mary by visiting Catholic churches. As Divine Mother in Self-Realization Fellowship gardens. As Kwan Yin in Oriental temples. As Shakti in Hindu tales. As White Buffalo Calf Woman in Native American teachings. A book here, an image there. But never enough. Where were the sacred mirrors of my feminine divinity? Why did the God of these times not have a feminine Beloved? Why was religious authority dominantly vested in the hands of men? Why Priests and no Priestesses? Why was there a void of feminine fluidity in art and architecture? Where were the feminine forces of cooperation and caring to balance masculine forces of competition and conflict? Why did so few even note the inequities of daily life?

ॐ

On the Fourth of July 1990, I declared my freedom from my fourth marriage and my intent to find answers to these questions. It was our fifth year of marriage, but Graham and I spent much of it apart to ease the tension between us. My physical and emotional health was severely depleted. Depression was a constant companion. Our relationship was fragmented and wounded. This relationship was *supposed to be* different. We were bonded in spirit. Our wedding ceremony had emanated Oneness and a Higher Love.

The "further information" that I had stayed open for after my October 1985 walk with God, had come from the Father. *Your work is complete. You may return Home . . . unless you choose to commit to staying on to assist in the work of closing the separating gap between men and women.*

Tired, weary and skeptical of my capabilities as I was, I answered aloud, "Oh, yes, dear Father. If you truly believe I can be of service. Yes. Yes."

Graham had come into my life that summer of '85 and it soon became clear we were to wed. Through marriage we would work to heal the separation. Everything in our lives felt miraculously orchestrated. But within six months, we had fallen into the abyss of all that was unholy between man and woman. The sense that our relationship was divinely ordained was so strong that we stayed together trying to obtain a holy relationship. Our life together appeared more and more unholy. We brought out the worst in each other and we were baffled and exhausted.

We had moved to Northern California, but were seldom together. That July Fourth, we were hoping to recapture what was good between us. Moments after I arrived, Graham shared a phone conversation he had just completed with a mutual friend. As he relayed their conversation about her spiritual crisis, I felt painful parallels. Frequently pondered inner questions surfaced. How could we have come together in a shared spiritual focus only to discover a vast spiritual void between us? How could I have experienced the Divine Oneness of the Mother/Father and feel such separation from my husband? How could I endure the pain of not knowing how to close the enormous gap between us? Why was I so inept in fulfilling my heart's desire to heal the sense of separation between women and men? Where had my health and vibrancy gone? What had happened during my marriage that warranted the comment from a new friend that I was the saddest looking woman she had ever seen?

My consciousness returned to Graham's voice as he said, "Ruth's feeling lost. I told her she'll find herself by reconnecting with God."

I started trembling. From the well spring of my being came the answer to my dilemma and hers. I stated with absolute knowingness, "She needs to reconnect with the Goddess to find herself."

He retorted, "God . . . Goddess . . . it's all the same."

It was not the same! At last I understood. To know myself, I had to know the Goddess! To understand my journey as a woman, I had to understand the journey of the Goddess for I was made in HER image and likeness. That day, I knew I must set out on the most important venture of my life. My energy was depleted due to my disconnection from my Goddess Self and I wanted to smile again!

Four months later, I joined with other women called by the Goddess to become Priestesses. When classes began on November 6, 1990, I felt a new level of commitment to living and to being the Goddess in Action. I felt wondrously nurtured and inspired simply sitting in the temple space among sacred objects honoring the feminine and nature. I absorbed Goddess energy into every pore of my being and gave thanks.

The program felt more like a reawakening of my Priestess Self than a training and I sensed I knew the other women from other times. The course was open to men, but unlike other sessions, none had enrolled. The diverse aspects of God were honored as the equal Divine Consort of the Goddess, but in order to bring forth balanced conscious awareness of the masculine and feminine aspects of deity, the Sacred Feminine was emphasized.

We only met one night a week, but the initiatory process began the moment I signed the enrollment papers. I know life as an initiation and often refer to my Higher Self as "CC," my Cosmic Choreographer. It became very clear, very early, that CC was going to superbly arrange every detail of daily life in preparing me for renewal of my ancient vows as a Priestess.

❧

The classes, the temple, the guidance of Lady Elena and Lord Kenneth kept me focused on the personal synchronicity of all life. Every aspect of my life was attuning to the mysteries of the Goddess wherever and however they were occurring. In addition to Temple of Isis rituals, I received inner guidance to participate in many of the women's ritual groups in Tucson. Once a month, I participated in the basement gathering at the Benedictine Sanctuary where nuns invited other women to join in casting a circle and calling in the Goddesses and the Four Directions. I knew the Mother Mary icons in the upper level sanctuary were smiling and I made greater peace with my past Catholicism. At New and Full Moon Ceremonies in the community, I reconnected to moon cycles and the rhythm of the Universe that we women have in our bodies, in our souls. When feeling off purpose, I went to the DeGrazia Foundation Chapel to visit Our Lady of Guadalupe who holds the Divine Blueprint for this region. The dark age of monotheism shrouding the many faces of the Goddess was ending and life was unfolding into a greater landscape.

All these activities were aspects of the larger curriculum as a Priestess candidate, but I needed to integrate them into a yet bigger context. Soon that opportunity presented itself. Late in January 1991, I returned to a southern California mountain community where I had lived during my last marriage to participate in a women's journaling retreat. I was happy to be back among these friends, but felt apprehensive about sharing my Priestess process with them. What if they did not understand or approve? To my surprise, the Catholic friend I thought might be most skeptical was very excited for me. Near the end of the powerfully bonding weekend, she tearfully declared loving support. "You have always been my Priestess. Now you are becoming a Priestess to the World."

I did not realize she was giving me a message from the Goddess that I would be ordained as a Priestess of Gaia, as a Priestess to the World. Nor did I realize that my work would be to assist in the mass awakening to the knowledge that each of us is Priest and Priestess to the World. But her words helped me more consciously attune to the devotion and love I have for Mother Earth. I began to realize the obvious. Gaia is the aspect, the face, of the Goddess closest to us all.

Back in Tucson, this Mother Earth/Earth Daughter relationship was painfully tested. Graham and I still shared stewardship of a sacred site on that mountain. He announced, by mail, that he was going to build there, disregarding my objections to developing the land. Suddenly, land we had held holy became a battlefield. I felt war torn. This land called VisionPoint was my body, my soul. It taught me Oneness. Taught me that all the Earth is a Sacred Site. The Deva, trees, plants, rocks, and creatures were my closest friends. It called to me across the miles to protect and honor its natural state. If I did not uphold my sacred trust as Priestess of VisionPoint, I could never become a Priestess of Gaia, the Earth Mother.

Simultaneously, war waged in the Mid-East. At home, I inwardly sought to achieve peace. I was hard on myself. I tended to live life competently, but kept failing in what I most wanted. Heart and soul, I wanted to achieve harmony between man and woman; harmony between humanity and nature. To succeed would be my greatest healing. To fail would be to live forever wounded.

War on the homefront was impacting all aspects of my life. My frustration and doubt were at an all time high. Reinforcements came, however. I returned to VisionPoint and did ceremony with a sister on Initiation Knoll. A Red-tailed Hawk dramatically swooped down to give me a message. *Trust the process. Trust the process.*

Weeks later, in the Temple, our class honored the local deity, Our Lady of Guadalupe. Lady Elena placed a statue of this Corn Mother in the middle of the room. Midway into the ceremony, I saw an etheric image of the Corn God next to the statue of Our Lady. The Corn God and Corn Goddess became lifelike and spoke to me. *Be patient. Trust the process. Ease up on yourself.*

I was now able to fully receive the message. Their Divine Presence signified that harmony between the masculine and feminine and all of nature would return. To live life on Earth in this context was the divinely designed blueprint that I chose to bring into form in this lifetime. I needed to trust that the outer conflict was simply the necessary surfacing of all that was untrue rising up for release and transmutation. *Trust the process. Trust the process.*

Fighting ceased in the middle-east. Ten days prior to my ordination a truce was reached regarding VisionPoint and sealed with a mutual commitment to seek Right Resolution. I had moved through the initiation. I gave thanks to VisionPoint, Graham, and the Corn God and Goddess for playing their parts in preparing me for the spiritually transformative experience of becoming a Priestess of Gaia.

&

As the months passed, my inner life became richer and more alive. Teachings and guidance were provided in the inner realms by Ladies Olivia and Elena, Lord Kenneth and Beloved Beings from other dimensions. In class, Lord Kenneth frequently stated that the Great Mysteries could only be understood when experienced on the Inner. This became vividly clear when he told the Creation Story of the Great Mother. Alone in the Garden she created life within her own being and gave birth to her Son, her masculine nature. I became the Goddess. I became the Garden. What beauty! What aliveness! Every cell of my body orgasmically awakened. The creative force danced in my body for many days and nights thereafter. Even now, the ecstasy returns when I recall the story. I now know why I feel so erotically alive alone in nature in what remains of the Garden.

Though my outer world had been largely devoid of Goddess mythology, I had identified with Athena, the Father's Daughter. Recently, I significantly changed that pattern by two means. First, I dropped my husband's last name in the divorce and did not reclaim my father's. Nicole Christine was now my legal full name. Second, I dedicated myself to the Mother in my Rio Grande rite and she revealed a new design for my life. Now it was time to for me to *truly understand* the Persephone and Demeter mystery. My Cosmic Choreographer set the stage at a "Wild Women's Weekend" produced by a women's ritual group. Here other stories of the Goddess triggered my deeply repressed grief, pain, and sadness around the death of my young mother when I was an infant. I had never tapped into my deep sense of abandonment. She had not been there to watch me grow or to guide me, and motherless like Persephone, I had to find my way alone in the underworld. I coped by relentlessly denying this emptiness until the Goddess arranged for a circle of twenty-two women to fill this void. When my agony unleashed itself, they held sacred space for me while I grieved uncontrollably. Then they filled the emptiness created by my release. They encircled me and caringly told me things my mother would have told me had she lived. It was as though the entire weekend was designed to assist me in reuniting the grieving inner daughter and mother. And I give thanks.

I supplemented my economic reserves and broadened community connections by facilitating journal writing workshops and private sessions. Fortunately, I did not need to take full employment during the initiation period. I was still rebuilding my health and staying focused on the inner work and keeping up with the related outer activities required considerable time, energy and attention. After completing my cycle as a caregiver, householder, and educator, I moved into a contemplative cycle. I loved Silence and a natural rhythm not ruled by clocks and calendars. Television, radio and newspapers did not define my reality, within or without. I held a clear intent to maximize the impact of my reawakening as a Priestess and I was very grateful for the way my consciousness was expanding.

Shortly before our Summer Solstice ordination ceremony, we were told it was customary to write a letter to Lady Olivia as a way of introducing her to the new Priests and Priestesses. We were to tell of our spiritual journey leading us to ordination in the Fellowship of Isis, evaluate the program, and indicate the triple aspects of the Goddess that we were dedicating ourselves to as Priestesses. Our letters would accompany one sent by Lady Elena and Lord Kenneth listing the newly ordained. I welcomed the assignment as a way to further integrate my process. A clear summation of experiences always enhanced my capacity to live more consciously. At the new moon, the time to seed the new, I eagerly sat down to write.

New Moon June 12, 1991
Tucson, Arizona USA

Lady Olivia Robertson
Clonegal Castle
Enniscorthy, Eire

Dear Lady Olivia,

It is an honor and a privilege to be writing this letter of introduction to you two weeks prior to my Full Moon ordination as a Priestess in the Fellowship of Isis. Until eight months ago, I had no conscious awareness of the Fellowship or of you and Reverend Lawrence. The dedicated work, you both have performed, is giving vital impetus to my life and the lives of many others. I am very grateful.

My journey to return to the Goddess does not seem to be a likely story to evolve out of the life of a child born into a large, extended Catholic family in a small Wisconsin Mississippi River town. But her parents of Irish/German and Slovakian heritage gave her a heathen name, 'Linda Lou' and appeased the church and relatives with the baptismal name 'Mary' in honor of the Virgin Mother. Was it thus preordained that she, as a woman, would first be ordained in the Madonna Ministry to bring forth the Feminine Aspect of Divinity through Mary; then ordained as a Priestess in devotion to the Great Goddess Isis of 10,000 faces?

Was there a soul agreement between her and her parents that would imbue a need within her to quest for a greater truth? Did her nineteen year old mother make her transition from the Earth plane while Linda Lou was in her infancy so that her heart and soul would always yearn for the mother beyond? Did her heartbroken father get sent off to war a year later and come back a wounded man so that the child would dedicate her life to World peace?

Did the struggles of her father and stepmother to sustain a marriage and family compel Linda to intently strive to achieve inner and outer balance of the masculine and feminine? If her parents had led an idyllic life, would she have stayed on the planet after walking with God and learning that her work for this lifetime was complete unless she chose to stay to assist in closing the gap separating men and women?

She ached for the freedom of going Home or of just living her own life after raising three half-brothers and two sons, experiencing three marriages, and giving what was left of herself to human rights and thousands of students. Yet, she embraced guidance to remarry believing that this man and she would bridge the gap together. But together, they discovered just how wide the gap was, within and without. And she came to know just how much the feminine was in need of healing and that she would not go Home until she was One with the Great Mother.

When this spiritually committed relationship ended in yet another divorce, she moved on alone. She was nearly swallowed up by the shadow of the relationship and realized she was a shadow carrier for men through

23

her bond with her father. Until she understood that this was all part of her training as a High Priestess who must hold the Balance of the Shadow and the Light, she lived with mounting fear that the shadow was victorious and she would never again be able to fully embrace the Light.

It is a blessing to write this letter. It is an opportunity to engage in needed reflection and weave together threads of my life which lead to the here and now . . . and to weave those threads into the greater tapestry of the Fellowship of Isis and the still greater tapestry of the Great Mystery.

This lifetime is the integration of many, many lives. Often, I feel as if I move into new lifetimes without needing to leave the body. I am clearing past negative karma with many people and reawakening to multitudinous identities with different races, cultures and spiritual affinities. Sometimes, I feel I am simply melding back into the Oneness and reclaiming fragmented parts of me as I return.

Native American spirituality and the Madonna Ministry, that sees nature as the bible and the Earth as our church, have helped me unite with Heaven and Earth. My developing Earth-centered spirituality was enhanced in the Priestess classes because of the way Lady Elena and Lord Kenneth hold space and offer guidance in the neo-pagan tradition.

The classes, overall, have been about reawakening the Priestess and the shaman I have been in many lifetimes. I am now ready to step forth as a Shaman Priestess ready to help birth a New Earth culture centered in spiritual ecology. I experience life as an ongoing initiatory process. The temple and College of Isis activities function keep me alert, on course and ever attentive to the inner realms.

I have awakened to the awareness that I am called to serve as a Priestess of Gaia. When I told this to a friend of some standing, her response was "What else could you possibly be?!" This triggers much emotion as I write because I am resistant to acknowledging to myself what has been so obvious about me to others. There is a fear I can not measure up. That I am not worthy or strong enough to co-create with our Beloved Earth Mother. In a past tribal life, I was not able to ward off the invasion of those who could not, would not, hold her as sacred. Oh, simply expressing that helps me release the residue of that lifetime and turn over my fears and doubts for healing and transmutation.

Earlier this year, another friend said, "You are becoming a Priestess to the World." A Priestess to the World. A Priestess of Gaia. Awesome responsibilities. Or is this simply an opportunity to step forth and acknowledge that each of us are becoming a Priest or Priestess of Mother Earth and Father Sky and that Earth is our temple and sky is its roof?

As Gaia heals and awakens to Her own destiny, I experience clear parallels to my own healing and awakening process. When I tap into feelings of being "taken for granted" as a giver and sustainer of life force energies, I know that we, the children of Earth, have adolescently taken our mother for granted. I then remember that she is moving forth on her own path and we all must realign with our individual and shared destinies.

Earth Mother's body is weary and worn from the journey and so is mine. As I work to regenerate physically, mentally, emotionally and spiritually, I am strengthened in knowing that this is what she is doing. As she heals, I heal. As I heal, she heals. She is becoming more conscious and so am I; so are we all.

I often experience Gaia's pain as my own. A sudden, excruciating searing in my stomach occurred when I rode past a mountain gorged for coal. I was traumatized by overwhelming grief and physical pain upon entering an area where a forest had been slaughtered to support the "Great American Dream." I feel raped and mutilated over the possibility of "development" of a site held in sacred stewardship by me for five years. I experience nightmarish images of a bulldozer clearing the land for a "home site" and feel my face and breast scraped off. The Earth and I cry out, "This can not be!"

I asked to understand the lesson. The answer is that this seeming dilemma is as much a part of my preparation for my Priestesshood as my childhood was. To tell VisionPoint's story is to tell Gaia's story, and ours.

The small, six acre site known as VisionPoint was ceremonially consecrated as holy by friends, my former husband, and me. It literally sits on the eastern edge of a Southern California mountain town where sun and moon rise up in the desert thousands of feet below. Here Mother Earth and Father Sky mate openly and the veil between the Worlds is thin. Guided by Mary, when ordained into the Madonna Ministry, I acknowledged VisionPoint as my church, my shrine, my holy land. I experience the land as my place of power, my teacher, my Beloved. Here Holy Spirit released Mary

Linda Lou and breathed life into Nicole Christine — so naming her to proclaim "victory to the people in Christed consciousness." I fully took on the vibration of this new name by making the change legal.

VisionPoint is the site of many personal rituals to the rising sun and the Four Directions. I, and many others, have been Initiated into higher planes of consciousness on Initiation Knoll that protrudes out toward the desert in full view by an elderly fundamentalist couple whose home sits above VisionPoint. Their presence helps me let go of the separation of differing beliefs because they, too, love the beauty and magic there.

As a Priestess of Gaia, I am to hold VisionPoint as sacred space until we all realize that all the Earth is sacred and live our lives accordingly. In other lives, I joined in ceremonies there to honor the sacred in All Life. VisionPoint is an ancestral ceremonial ground where we, the ancestors of tomorrow, gather in sacred space in small groups, in twos, or alone for giveback ceremonies, ritual, introspection and visioning. VisionPoint is an open gateway for the healing of the Earth, of our relationship to her, ourselves, and each other.

The potential secularization of this site serves as a microcosmic enactment of the dilemma between nature and "developmental man." At my ordination, I am lifting up a prayer for right resolution in this matter and fulfillment of VisionPoint's highest destiny. Whatever the outcome, I gratefully take all that VisionPoint and Gaia have given me into my being. I become one with their gifts that I may give them to others. I, as a Priestess of Gaia, desire to live and breathe the Sacredness of All Life. It is my intent to use my ability to express with the written and spoken word by doing more than speak of planetary and personal pain in hopes of preventing further destruction and possible extinction. I desire to proclaim the Beauty and wonder of Gaia and tell of her visions and truth as the Living, Loving Entity that she is.

White Buffalo Calf Woman is the second archetypal aspect of the Goddess that I am identifying with as an ordained Priestess. The White Buffalo has been a part of my inner reality for so long that I do not know when it first made its presence felt. When I learned what the Buffalo signified to the Lakota peoples, I felt full resonance. It was the greatest give-away from the Great Spirit, serving all the needs of the People . . . and White Buffalo energy always nourishes my soul.

Life has blessed me with the opportunity to walk with many indigenous people. In this way, White Buffalo Calf Woman has been the strongest aspect of the Goddess present to me throughout my womanhood. She has represented the Earth-centered spiritual nature of the Goddess Mary that the church of Rome tries to suppress. She brought the Peace Pipe to the People and embodies Peace on Earth. It is the returning time of this North American Goddess. As Priestess, I invite the energies of White Buffalo Calf Woman to forever flow through me. I vow to honor the Sisterhood of Woman Spirit at its highest level of Integrity and Unity. I dedicate my life to fulfilling my highest part in the rising up of the Earth Goddess and the realization of her highest destiny.

I will leave Tucson right after my ordination to travel for the summer. In my travels I will do the Dance of the People of the Heart to honor White Buffalo Calf Woman and the sacredness of the Earth and to reawaken my cells to the memory of oneness. This Dance to Mend the Sacred Hoop was once performed only in kivas by the medicine people. Recently, Elders of the Tsalagi (Eastern Cherokee Nation) gave it to Medicine Woman Dhyani Ywhahoo to take to "the people of this land to honor the quality of life and survival of the people." The lineage of my learning came through a dear sister, Catherine Friederich, who was taught by Choqosh Auh-Ho-Ho, a Chumash/Yaqui/Mayo Indian, who was taught by Dhyani.

The Triple Moon Goddess is the third archetypal aspect of the Goddess I am identifying with as a Priestess. As Grandmother to Gaia, she mirrors the triple aspects of the Earthly feminine energies: maiden, mother, crone. Through honoring her cycles, I honor myself and all women knowing that we, as women, have the rhythm of the Universe in our bodies. On a starlit night in April, in the Catalina Mountains near Tucson, I was ritualistically "croned" with a dozen other wise women and embraced the three aspects of the feminine. In so doing, I discovered that the maiden is more alive in me than ever. She now has the experience of giving to others as mother and the wisdom of fifty years of life fully lived.

As a Priestess of the Triple Moon Goddess, I vow to step forward in life realized as maiden/mother/crone doing my part to bring forth the re-emerging feminine into balance with the masculine warrior/father/elder. I seek this harmony within and without. I take this step consciously aware of the necessary activity of Mother Earth and all women during this period of planetary transformation to simultaneously be the Creatrix - giving new life; the Preserver - sustaining life; the Destroyer - eliminating all that is detrimental to Life's evolutionary progression. And I pledge, in response to the requests of the Grandmothers, to continue to place stone moon circles on the land wherever I travel. This is done to further anchor Grandmother Moon's energies on Earth. It is done and it is so. And I give thanks.

I also wish to acknowledge the Council of Goddesses that provides me with guidance, protection and love. This Council of Thirteen is convened by Beloved Kwan Yin, the deified personification of World Mother of Compassion. In the rest of the Circle sit Isis, Mary, White Buffalo Calf Woman, Gaia/Mother Earth, the Triple Moon Goddess, Diana/Artemis, Aphrodite/Venus, Our Lady of Guadalupe/Corn Mother/Tonantzin, the Black Madonna/ Kali/Pele, and the African Goddesses Oshun/Mother of Mountain and River, and Oya/Mother of Catastrophe – sudden structural change.

It is said that one should not approach Oya if you fear death, but approach her only if you fear not living a full life. The latter is my greatest fear. I have approached Oya with great respect asking that this fear be alleviated through the enactment of a life fully lived. Becoming a Priestess at this point in time and space is a vital statement of the intent to live life fully. I refused to live a partial life when I left my first marriage, the Catholic Church, and all the familial, social, religious, and cultural tradition therein. I recently read. "To go nine-tenths of the way is to suffer at every moment madness. To go all the way is to become totally sane." I know the madness when I resist "going the distance." In becoming a Priestess, I commit to total sanity, to going all the way.

As an Initiate of Mary, Virgin/Mother of God/Goddess of Wisdom through Peace, I am retaining my name Nicole Christine as a Gaian Priestess. As a magical name, in honor of our Earth Mother, I take the name "Laughing Brooke." This name holds the vibration of sparkling, dancing waters flowing as an individuated tributary, a bubbling lifestream of consciousness from the Mystic Mountains to the Great River of Life, Love and Compassion.

Laughing Brooke contains moon water essence, vibrantly dancing and flowing over and around rocks and fallen branches in a stream bed that gives form to her life yet alters to allow her course to change as her depth, breath and intent change with time and space. As Laughing Brooke, may my pure waters sparkle by day as the sun's rays penetrate me as I move. And by night, may my then shadowy movements capture and contain the Great New Mysteries that will be mirrored back to all who dare to look into the reflecting waters. As Laughing Brooke, I will welcome all Gaia's creatures that come to be refreshed in sacred waters even as I freely continue my Earth spirit journey as one of Nature's children, individuated and whole, in the natural order of All That Is.

In Dreamspace, Laughing Brooke's soul mate, Blake (B-lake = Brooke's lake), came to her in a harmonic blending of oneness far surpassing all of Nicole or Linda's fantasies of right relationship between the masculine and the feminine. In taking Laughing Brooke as a magical name, I proclaim that it contains the dynamic of Blake representing the male aspect of the female that I am. And, as Priestess, I wed these two components of Self in the Sacred Golden Marriage.

One of the aspects of the Priestess work with Lady Elena and Lord Kenneth, that I most value and appreciate, is the opportunity to experience their co-creative partnership on the material and spiritual planes. They are outwardly and inwardly doing much to close the gap between the masculine and the feminine and I honor them as forerunners in this most challenging endeavor.

It is clear to me that as an ordained Priestess, I will give my gifts as a communicator of the written and spoken word and as a group process facilitator in service to Gaia. I will honor the Sisterhood and perform the Dance to Mend the Sacred Hoop. I will create moon circles and honor moon cycles. However, it is not yet as clear how to do my part to heal the separation between men and women. I know I am to honor the God/Goddess aspects in Divine Union in all Creation and continue to heal myself. If I am guided to return to Tucson, I will continue to help build momentum for the Partnership Society movement that I helped activate here.

There is a clue for me in material I have been working with called the Gaia Matrix Oracle. I asked the oracle, "What is my purpose to which all my energies, resources and talents are to be dedicated?"

In response, I drew the archetypal card "Silver Net" that represents Cosmic Structure and the Spiritual Realization process of the Spiritual World in the New Earth. Part of the message stated, "The magnetic polarity of the sexes is refined through the heart, and the Queen (I read as Priestess) can help bride and groom realize that the first physical contacts must be actualized only out of the most expanded spiritual love. Otherwise the aura of the partners cannot access the true cosmic nourishment which will alone fulfill them." [3]

Long ago, I determined that the misqualification of the dynamic, co-creative sexual energy is key to discord between men and women and to the corresponding rape of women and the Earth Mother. In becoming a Priestess, I make the commitment to myself and to the Goddess to only engage in sexual activity actualized out of the most expanded spiritual love. And, when it is for the Highest Good, I will help others realize that this alone will fulfill them and will help restore the natural Beauty, Balance, Harmony and Abundant Fertility to our Mother the Earth. Blessed Be!

I thank you for reading my story. I did not expect to write so much. Lord Kenneth said that if we wrote ten pages you would read every word. I have almost done that! I believe you have absorbed every word and that, through my writing and your reading, my consciousness is crystallized and lifted higher. I am strengthened in my dedication to assist in cultivating humanity's highest co-creative potential and in authentically living from my vision point. I thank you!

In Joy & Celebration,
Nicole Christine/Laughing Brooke

6/24 Post Script: In preparation for ordination, Lady Elena and Lord Kenneth asked us to identify three aspects of the Goddess that we felt called to serve at this time and to determine which was the primary aspect. Gaia is clearly my primary aspect, but I had doubts about the other two because Venus also seems to be calling. Finally, I realized I am free to take four aspects. Four is the number of foundation and of Directions. Venus is to be my guide in my work to balance the feminine and the masculine. She and her Cosmic Consort Mars, presently performing a tremendous balancing act in the night skies, have been trying to draw my attention to this collaborative potential. I finally got the message! I had phenomenal experiences with Venus years ago at VisionPoint, and her addition at my ordination forms my Priestess Medicine Wheel. Venus is in the South, the place of Love. Gaia, in the West, the place where I work and where the sun will set on my life. White Buffalo Calf Woman, in the North, the place of the White Buffalo, my birth, and my hardest lessons. And Triple Moon Goddess in the East, the place I faced at VisionPoint when I experienced my first moon rise coming up out of the darkness way below me. I knew then that Life is magic. It Is Done. And So It Is. Blessed Be.

ॐ

A key aspect of my lifetime journey that I did not address in my letter to Lady Olivia was my role as a mother. That role was reactivated soon after the Priestess classes began because my oldest son lost his job in California. I found a larger apartment so Joel could come stay with me a while. In spring, when he was about ready to move back out on his own, Todd joined us. I had not imagined this occurring during my pilgrimage, but we clearly had unfinished business between us.

While marital dynamics tended to debilitate me, the role of mother was different. It was both my greatest challenge and my greatest reward for it stretched me in ways nothing else did. Mothering is an awesome privilege and a relentless responsibility. Loving and caring for these two beings, from their infancy to their adulthood, altered my perspective of time and space in ways no other experience has come close to doing. And no other experience generated as much joy and laughter or as many tears and fears as momhood did. The ups and downs of my sons' lives are primary motivational factors in my endeavors to help create a better world. Herein lies one of the greatest mysteries — the mystery of the Holy Madonna and Child. The mystery of a woman's charge to swaddle her young in a blanket of unconditional love and hold the immaculate concept of their divine perfection no matter what outpictures to the contrary.

In 1985, I made a special trip to an outdoor ocean shrine to Mother Mary just before escrow closed on our home. I placed an offering of flowers at her feet. "Mother," I said, "I have done all I know how to do to raise these two young men. We are going separate ways now. I release them to your loving care with deepest gratitude."

Walking away, I felt a great sense of relief knowing they were in her protective care. The response I had not waited for stopped me in my tracks. Her words were firm, yet loving. *I will watch over them, but remember you are my Earthly representative to them.*

Her reminder came to me many times in the following years. There was more mothering to do. And more letting go. This included letting go of fears that these sensitive young men would be crucified in the world and there would not be a resurrection for them or me. Six years later, I still had too much identity tied into being a mom and this was not good for any of us. The lease on my apartment was up shortly before my ordination. We made separate living arrangements. Once again, we were each going out on our own. I felt the straining lack of rites of passages for young people moving out into the world, and for mothers moving from their primary role as keeper-of-the nest into a new identity. The croning ritual had helped, but I needed to ritualize my intent to evolve from a caregiver at home and work-place to a Priestess to the World.

I created my own rite of passage. The moon was nearly full the night prior to my ordination. I cast a sacred circle around a large eucalyptus tree in the yard where I was house-sitting. Releasing a big sigh, I sat down and leaned against it. I was ready to die to all that had been that no longer served. Immediately, I felt the presence of indigenous ancestors. They held me in sacred space during my lengthy period of letting go of the past. When I finally felt emptied, I dug a hole and buried symbols of the past. Then, out loud, I read the obituary notice I had prepared.

On Tuesday night, June 25, 1991, Nicole Christine/Mary Linda Lou died to the pattern of daughter/wife/mother that she might be repatterned and reborn on Wednesday night, June 26, 1991. Her last request to those dear, and not dear, to her in the old pattern was that they release her. She asked them to sing her over, that she might become the more she is designed to be as a result of having committed to and been released from the pattern of daughter/wife/mother.

She did the best she knew how to do and it was good enough. And it is done. May she rest in peace and her body and soul be revitalized, repatterned into the dynamic lifestream to be known as Nicole Christine/Laughing Brooke . . . Priestess of Gaia, White Buffalo Woman, Triple Moon Goddess and Venus. It is done and it is so until it is appropriate for it to be otherwise. Blessed Be!

When the burial ceremony was complete, I lay myself on the grave. I declared, "I, Nicole Christine, of my own joyful volition, die to the daughter/wife/mother patterning and fully open to be reborn to the Priestess to the World patterning. SO BE IT!"

During the next twenty-four hours, I was in limbo. I had no identity, no attachments. And I, who had never missed a class, nearly missed my ordination by locking myself out of the house where the keys to the White Buffalo van lay. But then, it was a Full Moon and a Lunar Eclipse and I was between what I had been and what I was becoming. I was in the midst of a repatterning of all I had ever been throughout time.

I felt disoriented throughout the ordination. I went through the ceremony in a fog. But I did feel my soul take a quantum leap when I was
crowned Priestess of Gaia at One with Mother Earth. Gratitude and peace
filled my heart. It Was Done and It Was So.

ᏧᎳ

Reborn into a New Reality, I naturally needed to learn the new language.
In synchronistic perfection, six weeks prior to ordination, I participated in
a *Gaia Matrix Oracle* workshop. Rowena Pattee Kryder, the woman who
authored the Oracle, stated that as children of Gaia, we needed "to discover
and use the universal language that Gaia, as a living presence, uses to commune with her own body and to communicate with her children."[4] Hearing
these words, I knew that acquiring this language was my first major assignment as a Priestess of Gaia.

The Fellowship of Isis gives no directives or work assignments to its
ordained Priests and Priestesses who are encouraged to live their truth in
the world. Ordination confers ministerial status, but the "work" is between
one's Priest-ess self and one's God-dess aspects. Accordingly, three days after
my ordination, the White Buffalo and I were again on open road. We headed
for magnificent Mount Shasta in northern California where I would immerse
myself with others in a week-long *Gaia Matrix Oracle* (GMO) Intensive.
There was time en route to commune with Nature and old friends, but once
I arrived on the eighty acres of GMO land, I truly felt I was living a new
life in pristine beauty. Here I would camp and share and learn with people
who knew nothing of my past. The first night when we introduced ourselves,
I identified myself as a newly ordained Priestess of Gaia.

As the week progressed, we came to know ourselves, one another, and
Gaia deeply due to the influence of Old and New Earth archetypes accessed
via the card system of the Oracle. Midweek, I drew the Old Earth Death
Dance card for my soul archetype. Though I had already died to the old,
in mind and spirit, my soul had some clearing to do. We interacted with
the Oracle and one another through movement and drama in order to cellularly internalize the language. A Death Dance partner and I performed the
dance from the core of our beingness. I felt an immediate cellular repatterning take place within me that expanded for days as the Death Dance archetype furthered my transition into a new and heightened consciousness.

Each participant's final performance was to portray an integrated representation of what occurred individually throughout the week. Much of our
time was spent in a beautiful pine grove divided by a dry creek bed – *the
abyss!* Old Earth archetypes had domain over the south portion of the grove.
New Earth archetypes influenced the north portion. I felt pulled back and
forth between the Old Earth and the New, often straddling the abyss between
the two. The afternoon before final performance day I was released by the
purifying Old Earth Fulfilled Virgin/Child archetype, and embraced by Celestial Earth, a New Earth Fulfilled archetype.

33

At the close of that afternoon group activity, I felt called by the nearby stream. Soon, I stood barefoot in rapidly flowing waters and received my first ritual act as Priestess of Gaia. This ritual would be my final performance. The movements and words, incorporating the *Gaia Matrix Oracle* essence and symbols of the Virgin/Child and Celestial Earth archetypes, flowed through me in perfect resonance. Turning to the East, palms outward, I raised my arms and declared, "Be it known in the East, that I AM Nicole Christine, Priestess of Gaia. I AM Celestial Earth. My body is illumined. I AM one with Heaven and Earth. I give freely of my True Self for the Greatest Good of All and in a pure act of devotion co-creatively construct a New World Fulfilled in purity as Virgin of Virgins."[5]

I turned to the South, the West, the North, enacting the declaration rising up within me. Coming full circle, I took the pose of the pentacle star, the human image of Deity. With palms facing downward to ground the energies, I sealed the ritual with the words, "It Is Done and It Is So. Blessed BE."

That evening and again early in the morning, I repeated the ritual alone in the grove and over by the lake. It replayed in my waking and sleeping states and was becoming me - or I *it*. But that last afternoon in the grove with my GMO community, I grew anxious. I could not focus on the other presentations, though I was very interested in them. Always eager to participate, I had not been nervous during any other activities.

What was going on? I asked inwardly. Answers flooded forth. For years, I had done private rituals with utmost conviction. A decade earlier, after a *Zen realization* while washing my umpteenth sink full of dirty dishes, I began honoring the most mundane activities as sacred. But that was very personal and inward. Now I was going public. How presumptuous! In front of a dozen witnesses, I would declare my intention to lift myself out of the abyss of reactivity and the quagmire of projections, obsessions, and addictions to committedly and co-operatively co-create a pristine New Reality! Was I really ready to let go of my *stuff* and surrender to a Higher Truth? Was I capable of making a difference?

Separate and alone, the answer was "no." In the Oneness, the answer was YES! I acknowledged my fears, blessed and released them. Moments later, when we took a watermelon break, I asked my Death Dance partner and another close new friend for support. They lovingly, compassionately, gave it. Rowena asked, "Who's next?"

I answered, "I am."

I asked the group to form a circle with me in the New Earth part of the grove. I spoke of my anxieties and asked for support that freely poured forth. Strengthened, I rose and made my declaration to the Four Directions. I felt transformed by every word, every movement. Then I moved around the circle making eye contact and naming each individual as I stated, "Be it known in the Four Directions that you (name), are Celestial Earth. Your body is illumined. You are one with Heaven and Earth. Give freely of your

True Self for the Greatest Good of All and in a pure act of devotion co-creatively construct a New World Fulfilled in purity as Virgin of Virgins."

When I completed the circle, I knew that everyone, everywhere, is a co-creator with the New Earth. We are the celestial Priests and Priestesses at One with the Living Gaia, our Mother Earth, and with All Life. A sister stood and said, "I, too, have been feeling afraid. I am ready now to give freely of my True Self." I was humbled by the mystery and magnitude of what was evolving in the Universe and I gave thanks.

૪

Some of us stayed on after the intensive to integrate. Near the end of the second week, I had the entire place to myself while others went river rafting. I committed to water the gardens and feed the cat. I embraced the solitude. There was so much to absorb about the intensive, my ordination, my entire pilgrimage. Plus, my body was simply exhausted. Surviving in the Old Earth and getting to the New had been very hard work and my body vehicle felt very much like an Old Earth model.

I was quite concerned about my health. I experienced a sudden weight loss and had a growing lump in my right breast. Alone on the land, I made an earnest call to the Universe for answers about my body. On my third morning alone . . . in the garden . . . eating freshly picked snow peas . . . feeling the ecstasy of oneness with life . . . thinking that this was the true way to live. . . . Suddenly, I telepathically heard, *You have lymph cancer throughout your system. You do not have long to live.*

Stunned, I was muted and immobilized for hours. Tears streamed forth from some well-spring deep inside me. It was my body's turn to die. Was it literal? How could that be? Was stepping onto the banks of the New Earth all there was to be for me? Questions that could have insanely riddled my mind surfaced only to be washed away by my constant waterfall of tears. And so it was throughout the day and into evening . . . not knowing if this death would be symbolic or actual. At nightfall, I sat at the table in the community kitchen and began journaling in hope of achieving clarity. I wrote for hours always coming back to the same conclusion. If I am to die, I want to die consciously. If I am to live, I want to live consciously. Either way, FULL consciousness was required. If I could consciously die to all that was killing me, I could do so without leaving my body. If I could let go of all my fears of death, I could truly live in a New Earth body. Or so it seemed. . . .

I was so tired. So very tired. But much too restless to sleep. This was the best performance of my Cosmic Choreographer yet! It was so convincing. Was it going to be curtains for me soon. I turned to the Oracle for comfort and insight and drew The Blue Pharaoh, an archetypal card new to me. Cautiously, I turned to the corresponding reading. . . .

THE BLUE PHARAOH represents your power to pass through
death experiences or pass through matter with your
electronic body.
Be aware of your nerve centers and use your wakefulness
towards the immutability of the spirit.
Trust the quality of your spirit and be aware of the
temporary garment of matter
as an opportunity to develop a light-body.
It is by the reverse process of growth through dying that
the seed-crystal of your light-body will be born.
Cease being tempted by externals and humbly commit
yourself to allowing a death and a new, higher vibration
vehicle to be born within you. [6]

I read in wide-eyed amazement and when I finished I felt all traces of
old thought systems begin to crumble. Feeling I had nothing to hang onto,
I cautiously made my way to the White Buffalo where I collapsed into sleep
that continued well into the new day.

૨⋅

I left the Mount Shasta area a few days later and headed an hour south
to Redding where I lived prior to my pilgrimage. In the days and weeks
that followed, I did not know if I was dying or transforming into my light
body. Even though I understood that I had to psychically die to accomplish
the latter, it all seemed crazy. And yet, my life had never felt so clearly
guided. I knew when to talk about the death and when to keep quiet. I was
blessed by shelter with a friend very supportive of my process. She told me
of a massage therapist who had a similar inner experience and healed her
breast cancer. The woman transformed in consciousness in the process as
she discovered a new, higher vibrational relationship with her physical, mental, emotional, and spiritual bodies. We met and she helped me affirm my
surrender to the Greatest Good, be that to live or to die, leaving this body
behind with Gaia.

If I was to literally die, I wanted to do so at VisionPoint. If I was going
to transform, I knew no better place to do so. VisionPoint was the ocean
of my being. I headed further south early in August feeling much like a
turtle heading back to the sea to die.

It was good to be on the road. Long distance driving and personal
journaling were my most effective ways to commune with my True Self who
would reveal my Inner Healer. My journal was my bible and by writing out
my deepest thoughts and feelings in it, I was better able to face death and
to live more fully. My journal was a tool of empowerment. I was coming
to know myself more accurately and deepen my connection to the Great
Spirit, which spoke to me now as the Great Mother, the Great Nurturer, I
so needed.

In a Redding bookstore, the popular novel *Dying Young*[7] caught my eye. Hesitantly, I decided to purchase it. Minutes later, in another section of the store, another book fell into my hands - *SHE LIVES! The Return of Our Great Mother*. I claimed this book eagerly! I began reading them both and routinely did the Healing Meditations of Our Great Mother. I used a meditation line as a mantra to affirm my healing while gently and lovingly cupping my breasts with my hands. "Oh, Great Mother, bless and heal my breasts that, like Thee, I may nurture myself and others." This simple act did much to help me feel whole, connected to my body, to Spirit, to all Life.

But the fears of *dying young,* and of facing the issues still around VisionPoint that would have to be addressed when I arrived there, were very intense the last morning in my friend's home. Restlessly awake, several hours before my departure, I turned to the Great Mother in my journal and wrote, quoting again from the book *She Lives!*[8]

Oh, Great Mother . . . please help me move through my fears concerning the next phase of the journey. I want to replace my fear with faith for You art with me. Your Words shall be my words and the shadow of dis-ease shall no longer have dominion over me. Oh, Great Mother, bring light into this darkness. "You are all creation, all intellect, knowledge and wisdom. You bring the eternal light, may we be reconciled with You. Many are the gods, but You, Great Mother, are One." Your love is with me always from the beginning of time. And as You are in me, so I am in You, complete and whole. And I give thanks.

When I put down my pen, I felt peaceful enough to sleep until dawn. I was on the road soon after awakening. Early that evening, I arrived at the Stanislaus National Forest just west of Yosemite. Following a quick campsite supper and a walk by the stream, I felt ready for sleep before it was fully dark. I read more of the return of Our Great Mother and was moved to acknowledge love for myself. Warmly embracing myself inside my sleeping bag, I drifted into welcomed slumber.

Chilled by the early dawn, I awoke and grabbed my jacket. I snuggled back deeply into my sleeping bag after communicating with Grandmother Moon a bit. Slowly, gently, I felt enveloped by and with Love of and for The Great Mother. Tears flowed with the blessing. I heard her say, *I love you, Nicole. You are a very good person. You have done well with Life. You deserve love. Deserve to be cherished. I cherish you. I honor you. You deserve well being, health, vitality, comfort, acknowledgment, companionship, a mate and partner.*

How the tears came! I shook. I felt my heart chakra expand, hurting a bit in the process. Heat flooded the left side of my body and I felt greater balance. Suddenly, energized, I quickly got behind the wheel, still wearing my sleeping sweats, and headed for Yosemite to absorb its wondrous beauty before the flow of human traffic advanced.

My drive east through the park and south down Highway 395 took me to Diaz Lake by nightfall. It had been a very good day. The drive through sparsely populated countryside helped me continue to clear. Just before turning in for the night, I finished reading *Dying Young*, then again communicated to Our Great Mother in my journal. . . .

Oh, Great Mother . . . I do not want to die. I do not want to have cancer or any other debilitating dis-ease. I want to be a vessel of Thy Wholeness, Beauty and Wonder . . . Perfect and Complete in You. But I surrender to the Greatest Good for All in Thy Perfection. Please be with, in, and of me in the weeks ahead in relating to VisionPoint matters and to You. Please help me disengage from dual mind, from the quagmire of Old Earth codependency and insanity. I dedicate all my thoughts, deeds and actions to Truth, to Thee, Divine Mother.

Devotedly, Your Daughter, Nicole Christine

ॐ

Nothing existed but the moment whenever I stood on the mountain at VisionPoint gazing eastwardly over the vast desert into eternity. This was truer than ever upon this return. All of creation felt vibrant, alive. Deva, the nature spirits, the birds, the pines, the wild flowers and manzanitas, the wind and sun, rejoiced in my presence and I in theirs. It was very good to be alive on Planet Earth!

During my two-month stay on the mountain, everything and everyone felt more crisply alive and real. Why, I wondered, do we feel most alive near death? Why do we take life for granted until we think we might no longer experience it? I wanted this aliveness all the time without the seeming loneliness of death. To keep from feeling so alone in dying, I talked openly with some of my old community of friends. To keep from feeling life was over, I did not tell others, needing them to relate to me *as usual*. In both cases, I became keenly aware of how blessed I was by the richness of so many loving people. I opened to receive the love and support I had often deflected in my old *I'll make it on my own!* stance.

Much of August, I stayed in a friend's cabin where I could rest and eat well, but I camped at VisionPoint in the White Buffalo with frequency. In September, I lived in a magical windmill when I was not on the land. The Universe provided me with what I needed in effortless, life-sustaining ways. One friend gave me free dental care "as an ordination gift." A new *Gaia Matrix Oracle* friend sent me a check for $200 for health care services. In receiving, there was a natural ebb and flow of ways I could give back in heartfelt appreciation.

Feeling cared for helped me to clearly see through the eyes of a Priestess to the World. I realized that by tapping into the consciousness of being cared for as a Priestess, within temple walls in lifetimes past, and transferring that into consciousness of the world as the temple, all I needed to fulfill my highest destiny would be provided.

Only my belief in lack and limitation and my expectations of how what would come to me blocked the natural flow of universal abundance into my life — be it appropriate wealth or vibrant health. Having experienced the art of living hand-to-mouth early in life, I had a basic belief that I would always survive economically. I was not so confident in terms of my health.

I tried working through health blockages by having a traditional medical exam and blood tests. I soon halted this approach. I did not have insurance and did not want to tap the Universe for funds for such an unnatural, impersonal, and invasive process. I chose not to have a mammogram, a biopsy, or surgery. Medical man was quick to cut people just as developmental man was quick to cut up Earth Mother and disrupt the very ecological systems that sustained man, woman, and child. Because we are spiritual beings, we and Earth have the power of regeneration within us and can heal if our natural powers are supported instead of disruptively invaded.

I would seek more natural forms of assistance from healing facilitators. I would do the work I needed to do to heal myself. And as I healed, so would the Earth Mother. As she healed, so would I. The more I did to heal and respect my body, the more Earth would heal and respect me. The more I did to heal and respect Earth, the more I would heal and respect myself. By learning to love Gaia and myself as One, the World and All That Is would move closer to wholeness.

I have long believed in a direct correlation between *female problems* and *Earth problems*. Each woman with a tipped uterus mirrors Earth Mother's tipped axis that mirrors the tipped consciousness of humanity. Each woman raped reflects the recurring rape of our Mother Earth reflecting the rapist consciousness of the species. As we heal, the uterus and the axis will be righted and there will be an end to rape in all forms.

I believe that my own *breast problem* is associated with a lack of nurture due to separation from the Mother and my correspondingly depleted ability to nurture myself and others. What self-love either my former husband or I had was severely battered in our marriage. He had moved back to the mountain. When we met at VisionPoint, it was clear that my physical recovery required emotional recovery and our shared love for the land was containing us so we would do the work of healing. We had held open the possibility of reuniting in a less enmeshed way after my pilgrimage, but it was obvious that would not occur. Now we had to ascertain what to do about our shared ownership in the context of separate lives.

The possibility of my death complicated the resolution process. This heightened the confusion we often felt because we shared an extraordinary inner reality and a highly dysfunctional outer one. Sometimes I felt crazy trying to cope with this dilemma. So crazy that my physical body replicated the turmoil of my emotional and mental bodies. Cancer is cells gone crazy, cells that are highly dysfunctional.

We argued. We laughed. We cried. We broke through a barrier only to crash into another. One spoke from the inner dimension where our True Selves shared a vision and held each other, the land, the World, in holy regard. The other mockingly latched onto a destructive pattern in our outer world that confirmed we were incapable of holding anything in joint stewardship.

Though VisionPoint nurtured me and we progressed on many levels, the process was draining too much of my life force. Alone there for an extended period, I knew I would be renewed, but the early fall nights were getting too cold to make van living feasible. I asked for Guidance. *Return to Tucson.* There I could get the alternative health care I wanted. There I had numerous creative and spiritual outlets that would fire my passion to live. There I had my sons whose very existence had often been my prime reason to live. There I could economically support myself in ways not possible on the mountain.

This decision meant leaving without achieving resolution around Vision-Point. Developing the land was still an unacceptable consideration to me. This was a ceremonial ground. Here humanity, the ancestors, the critters, the Directions, the Elements, the Earth and Sky sacredly merged into the Oneness where we truly know our co-creative roles in the ongoing process of Creation.

On August 17, a number of us had gathered at VisionPoint to honor the fifth anniversary of the Harmonic Convergence. Like millions around the planet, we came to anchor the cosmic outpouring of the energies of divine self-governance. The next day was the beginning of the end of the Soviet Union.

On the eve of the August Full Moon, alone on Initiation Knoll with its 360 degree view, I danced with the wind and completed the nine rounds of the Dance to Mend the Sacred Hoop. And there I returned at dawn to greet the rising sun and pay homage to the Four Directions. That night, in the cradled hallow below the knoll, I danced and sang in the shadows around my moon circle. Grandmother Moon, in her fullness, cast an enchanting silvery glow on me and my brothers and sisters – the rocks, the trees, the plants. I called out to the Great Mother, "Please assist me in fulfilling my highest destiny moment-to-moment."

For several years, my highest sense of destiny seemed intertwined with VisionPoint and the man I had married. Graham had always wanted to build there. I would always want to leave the land as it is. We had, though, shared the vision of a butterfly garden we would co-create with each other and the nature spirits. Nature was not waiting for us to resolve our differences. She had already created the garden. Wild yellow flowering shrubs blossomed boldly and butterflies fluttered everywhere.

Was the vision now complete? Would dying be the resolution? In making rounds of good-byes with mountain friends and places, I fully expressed my love and respect for each so I would not leave anything of value unsaid before departure. It was now early October 1991. I completed the last two days of my year of pilgrimage in solitude. My last night on the mountain was spent at VisionPoint in communion with the Great Mother.

The moon was new. The night was dark. My soul was illumined by the understanding that in facing my fear of death, in surrendering to life's cycles, I had undergone the waning moon initiation of the High Priestess who knows the dark. Now I could be reborn with the waxing moon. In dreamtime, I traveled deep into the inner realms that night; and when I awakened, I performed my final ritual in the heart space of VisionPoint.

Direction by Direction, I turned to affirm. . . . *I AM Nicole Christine, Priestess of VisionPoint, Priestess of Gaia, High Priestess of the Great Mother. I AM Celestial Earth. My body is illumined and I AM one with Heaven and Earth. I give freely of my True Self for the Greatest Good of All, and in a pure act of devotion, co-creatively construct a New Earth Fulfilled in purity as Virgin of Virgins. It Is Done and It Is So. Blessed BE.*

❦

It is now late January 1992. Truly a new beginning! I am lovingly, playfully, embraced by Life in Tucson. Vibrant joy and laughter bubble up within me. Much of the time life feels extraordinary. Other times, comfortably ordinary. My body is still weak. I still feel there is little time left to this lifespan. But right now, I am very much alive!

I live in an enchanting, tiny adobe house just west of town. Here some of the desert remains intact and gives witness to sunrise and sunset. Though there are other houses nearby, mine is situated so I rarely see people. My companions are cactus wren, hummingbirds, thrashers, quails, sparrows, cardinals, cottontail and jack rabbits, coyotes and javalinas. Many of my days are spent observing and communing with them. A good deal of my evening time is spent by the fire.

This is my womb space, my chrysalis. Here I am learning to truly nurture and love myself. For the first time in my life, I have a place of my own that is simply about and for me. Everything in this space is a mirroring statement of who I am right now in my life. I like what I see. The space is perfect for my healing. This space in the West, the Direction of assimilation of all karmic and life experiences, the doorway to ego death and yearning for full mergence with spiritual consciousness.[9]

One evening by the fire, after a lovingly prepared, nourishing, candlelit meal, my Inner Healer told me that dis-ease was leaving my body proportional to how much I nurtured and cared for myself. This simple activity of self-love has been a long time coming, and I rejoice in its arrival. I give myself the time and attention I have, in neediness, yearned for from a mate. I give myself the time and attention I have given to others in my outer directedness. And I am replenished and have more to give and receive. This is resulting in a strong, centering sense of balance. This is creating a lifestyle of healthy, stimulating outer activities balanced with healthy, self-nurturing solitude and contemplation. Everything I do now is inner directed and organic to my personal process, which is an extraordinary liberation from the controlling demands and expectations I assumed the outer World wanted from me.

When I was settled in my space, I received persistent guidance to get ALL my affairs in order. To live in a **clean, clear, current** way so that I leave no clutter, no unfinished business, or unresolved relationships behind. Achieving this has been magical. The simple act of updating my will required the ordering of many details in my life. It became playfully challenging to be sure there was not a single piece of paper in my files that was not relevant to life now, not a single item of clothing that did not have purpose, or a single book or dish on my shelves that did not belong in my life now. I was in conscious relationship with everything in my life and very present in the moment.

NOW. NOW. NOW. In preparing for the possibility of dying, I was learning to truly live here and now. I was becoming dynamically in touch with the moment. I cleared away the internal and external **busyness** and became fully present in the moment, which is all there really is. Anything short of this is walking death, for life force is consumed by what was or what might be. Life force flourishes in the moment and incorporates the past, present and future in the totality of the moment. The more current I was, the more Current flowed through me.

The key to accomplishing this state of *being present* was to eliminate all stress from my life because it was literally killing me. I set appropriate boundaries with my sons and friends and found freer, lighter ways of relating. I consciously prepared healthy foods. I sought out natural health care practitioners to assist in my healing process. I became increasingly attentive to my body's natural intelligence and my Inner Healer's innate sense of what I needed to do, how and when. Most of all, I let go, let go, let go. . .

This meant owning my anger, pain, hate, sadness and fears and forgivingly moving through it all into clarity, healing, love, joy, and safety. In the process of creating order and eliminating stress in my emotional, mental, physical and spiritual houses, I kept coming back to the same reality. The major source of stress was rooted in the ongoing effort to reach resolution with Graham about VisionPoint. Though we had parted optimistically, it felt absurd to try to work out, long distance, what we could not work out in two months on the mountain together, what we could not resolve in a six-year relationship.

When I expressed my anxiety and need for closure to him, more stress was generated, eventually followed by more letting go and more healing. Given I just might be staying alive a bit longer, I wanted, needed, to get on with what life was opening up for me. I had no energy to keep trying to co-orchestrate a vision of what could be. IF we could work things out, a projected plan had been that I would return to the land in the spring and live in a yurt while we co-created the butterfly garden. But the *things* we

needed to work out amounted to our ongoing issues about money, partnering, priorities, trust, whose codependency *stuff* was whose, et cetera, et cetera.
Whenever I turned my attention to those *things*, life force drained out of
me. Whenever I stayed fully present in life in Tucson, I felt vibrantly alive.
And I wanted to live!

So I let go of the vision. I let go of VisionPoint only to fully realize I
AM VisionPoint. No matter where I am or what I do in the outer, that vision,
that land, will always be alive for me in the inner planes. And if the land,
my partner there, and I are to share an ongoing outer plane destiny, it will
unfold naturally and not through frustrated or hopeful projections on my
part or his. For now, there were many doors opening for me in Tucson and
I had not explored them on the chance I would leave in the spring. The
holding back was stressful. I needed the ease of going with the flow.

For a while, I let myself feel distraught. Was I, in letting go, failing
VisionPoint, settling for a lesser destiny, giving up hope of bringing the
spiritual partnership I knew on the inner, forth into the outer dimension?
Blah, blah, blah! While in the throes of doubt, I was awakened one morning
with guidance to see Lady Elena and Lord Kenneth. They made time to see
me that afternoon. We had not gotten together since my return and it was
a good reconnection. They were attuned to psychic death and offered valuable insight into what was going on with me. Then as they shared changes
they were going through, I became more aware of how their spiritual work
and daily lives were one and the same. My heart's desire that this also be
true for me surfaced for re-examination.

Our visit triggered my awakening to the Priestess of Gaia work ahead
for me. My external interactions with them tended to be minimal, but, occasionally, I would tune into a deep, collaborative relationship on the Inner
where we helped etherically keep the Fellowship of Isis activated for thousands of years. Now it was time for me, like them, to do my part to enhance
the re-emergence on the outer plane.

In the days and nights that followed, I moved in and out of a dreamtime
dimension where a Gaia Temple and Institute exist for the purpose of in-
itiating Priests and Priestesses to the World. There I live, move, and have
my being as a High Priestess fulfilling my highest destiny at this point in
this planet's evolutionary spiraling process of creation. There are many vari-
ables to be played out before it becomes possible for this to be enacted on
this physical plane, and writing this work is one of the factors.

During the last class, Lady Elena delivered a message from the Goddess.
She said I would write a doctoral discourse and receive a Doctorate of
Divinity Degree through the Fellowship in the near future. I resonated with
her words and even knew the theme would be on Priests and Priestesses
to the World. But at that time, I was much more interested in gypsying for
the summer than in taking on any such project.

I thought about the doctoral work after resettling in Tucson, but still
had no interest in writing anything. After our talk, however, I realized the

paper was needed to bring the blueprint of the Sacred Work from the etheric to the physical realm by committing it to written form. My excitement grew, then dissipated as I began resisting due to old ways of thinking. This was too far-fetched. It would take energy I did not have. I was tired of being on the cutting edge of consciousness. I just wanted to BE. There was no way two Goddess Centers could survive in the same town. Et cetera and so on.

Clearly, I had more to work through in myself before I could begin to write. I needed to integrate the fragmented aspects of my consciousness. I recognize everyone in my world as a mirrored aspect of myself and know that whenever I experience separation, I have found a place in me where I feel less than whole. I wanted to disown this awareness in terms of Graham, resisting the possibility that his behaviors that most upset me might be mirroring qualities I do not like in myself. My healing advanced when I realized that the qualities I loved and admired in him were also qualities in me that he was mirroring. These, too, wanted to be integrated as aspects of my multi-dimensional self. In doing so, I began to know my inner male better and grasp what I need to do to heal my masculine aspect.

Still I resisted writing. I asked Gaia for help. And help she did. In the midst of the holidays with 1991 nearing an end, I experienced a healing, catalyzed by a written communication from Graham. It literally lifted the debilitating stress I stored in my body during our relationship, and permeated my being with lightness. Two days later, while celebrating Christmas with my sons, I experienced a healing shift in relationship with these long-term mirrors of my inner male. We were a family again **and** independently unique beings.

A few days after Christmas, reading the late arriving annual Christmas letter from my parents, I moved through a stepdaughter/stepmother variation of Persephone and Demeter. I tapped into my grief that, though my stepmom had come into my life while I was still young, we had not bonded emotionally. I felt a loss for never experiencing familial intimacy with a mother or sisters or daughters. She had not been the *wicked stepmother*. She was yet another unsung being, who takes a child she did not conceive and treated it as her own. There were simply economic factors causing her to work outside the home leaving little time for mother/daughter bonding. I understood this intellectually, but I had never touched the deep pain and sadness that time and distance and perspective separated us so definitively. I grieved, then moved into that inner place of oneness where I did my healing the inner child work. I invited my stepmom to merge into me to heal the inner mother/daughter split so that my fragmented feminine aspect could become whole. We merged. Separation dropped away. My love and appreciation for her could live.

ᨑ

I felt intensely good about the caliber of inner work I had completed by year's end and I moved into the new year filled with exhilaration. But I felt even less like writing. On New Year's Eve, I drew *The Fool* card from the *Gaia Matrix Oracle* deck as my archetypal influence for 1992! I was elated about the implied freedom-to-frolic! It was time to play after a lifetime of hard work before taking on a new project, even for the Goddess. I wanted to attract a playmate lover, a Fool Priest (living in his own space!), to intimately share and spontaneously explore life with a Fool Priestess.

However, contrary to old patterns of jumping in, I let the attractions I felt toward men play themselves out on the inner. Thus I did not outwardly expend energy I needed for myself. I related each attraction or repulsion I felt toward a man to my commitment to call in and merge with the fragmented parts of my masculine self. I wanted to stop projecting my animus onto men and more fully be a woman, a virgin again, whole unto herself. Then I could, in divine timing, magnetize a man whole unto himself.

It was a casual call from a friend that generated my enthusiasm for writing the doctoral paper. I had not discussed the paper or the Priestess to the World work with others, but as Bridget and I talked, I realized that she was one of the Priestesses. I timidly put forth the concept and she excitedly indicated her strong desire to be an ordained Priestess. She had recently been thinking of the tradition nuns had of marrying themselves to Christ and thought that now is the time to marry the Earth. Our conversation came to life with unrestrained, shared excitement about our inner awareness. She had even been thinking about Green Man who was a delightfully merging component of my unfolding process. Motivated by our talk, I committed to organize my affairs so I could begin writing within a few days.

The next evening, I risked sharing a bit more with another friend, Maya, who came by for supper. She, too, was responsive. Much of our talk revolved around my need to bring forth, through ordination, my inner High Priestess commitment to the Great Mother and my sense that the present day connotation of *High* was separating. Even though *high* means working with a *higher vibration*, rather than being *higher than* others, I felt new languaging was needed for these times. I needed to bring forth New Earth concepts and language. We explored ideas, but reached no conclusions.

The next morning I experienced the sought-after *aha!* This was the insight I needed to open the floodgates of what wanted to be written. The guidance was to become a *Crystal* Priestess of Gaia because the essence of my work is to express the crystalline qualities of the Earth Mother. Other ordained Priests or Priestesses to the World, choosing further initiation, would work toward expressing the prime Earth quality contained in their nature. When they knew themselves well enough to name themselves, they might be ordained as an Emerald or Raven Priest or an Owl or Willow Priestess. This tradition rises up through the mysticism of native peoples in this land. High Priestess comes through the Egyptian mysteries. I knew, loved, and honored both traditions.

This realization was empowering. Numerous pieces of my personal puzzle, loose threads in my personal tapestry, fragmented aspects of my nature, trail markings on my path, merged into a crystalline whole. The very act of writing the doctoral paper was my initiatory preparation as a Crystal Priestess of Gaia. The process challenged me to become very clear about experiences and understandings of endless lifetimes and how to integratively actualize them in this lifetime.

Persons who read auras and energy fields have told me that I have a crystalline core that is highly charged and highly reflective. Writings by Graham tell of our shared 700,000 year journey through time and space. He speaks of me as Chrisenteel, a consciousness that emerged from the crystalline core of VisionPoint. I have a strong affinity with my Capricorn quartz crystal birthstone and an insatiable desire for clarity in all aspects of my life. I **need** clear, clean windows. I keep my foods in clear, usually glass, containers to have direct relationship to food uncontaminated by marketing propaganda. I rarely read newspapers to avoid clouding my perceptions of Life with mistaken projections of mass consciousness. I spend most of my alone time in Silence. No television. No radio. When I play music, it is for dancing or to vibrationally lift my spirits. For me, Silence is one of the most sacred aspects of Life assisting me in maintaining a crystal clear connection with Source, Nature, and All My Relations.

To be a Crystal Priestess is to be so clear in spirit, mind, body and soul that it is no longer possible to be manipulated or entrapped by outside energies. It means being a clear channel of Divine Love and Power uncontaminated by identity, ego, persona, yet uniquely individuated. It means seeing beyond the obvious into the deeper meaning of things and consciously, simultaneously, living in multi-dimensional planes. It means carrying no shield or protective amulet, knowing violations are not possible in the realms of clarity. This clarity is the aspect of the Great Mystery I chose to master in this lifetime. It is my reason for being. It is the way in which I am to serve.

The multi-dimensional aspects of reality are becoming clearer moment-to-moment. The confusion of having a relationship vibrantly harmonic on the inner and discordantly conflictive on the outer has dropped away. Souls do the work they need to do, have the experiences they need to have, on many planes of existence until they simply feel finished. Graham and I danced in the shadows together **because** of the inner realm commitment we made to assist in each other's outer realm evolution.

Now I am dying as that which is outworn continuously does. I am living forever as I always have. I am actively involved in the Gaia Temple and School on the inner with many people I see frequently in very ordinary worldly roles. If I leave this physical body, I will continue this involvement, and the involvement with VisionPoint in my etheric body. If I stay in this body awhile longer, I may be guided to manifest the temple and school on this plane for the remainder of this decade. By the year 2000, humanity will be conscious that they are Priests/Priestesses, stewards, and co-creators to and with the Earth, and no such formalized activities or structures will be needed. The thoughtform of the Priest and Priestess to the World will be so internalized that this consciousness will manifest everywhere in everyone in everything we do, feel, say.

The veil between dimensions is getting thin. I went to a gathering at an adobe house that was much like the temple and school structure I see on the inner. This house is not *it*, but I now have a concretized third dimensional image to assist me in grounding energies activated on the inner. Further, I am comfortably aware of many others whose work complements the work I am guided to pursue.

I see it all happening effortlessly, organically. This is an enjoyable, welcomed lesson! If something takes efforts and drains my energy, I am not to do it — at least in that time and that way. What occurs effortlessly indicates I am fully conscious and in the natural flow of life. When I insist on efforting, everything in my life gets out of sync. Crystal clarity is required to know the difference between passivity and active receptivity, between impetuousness and spontaneity, between flowing with the current and being washed downstream.

I am fascinated by the emergence of Green Man in this process. Looking to the matrix of a college, shop, and temple manifesting through Lady Elena and Lord Kenneth, I understood my equivalency would be Earth Song Institute, Earth Song Shop, and the Temple of Gaia. Knowing it is time for the return of God/Goddess consciousness, Gaia had to have a male counterpart honored in the temple. But what was the appropriate aspect of male spirituality, God, divine consort, needing expression in this work?

Awareness of Green Man had been faintly filtering into my consciousness for over a year, pressing forth strongly when I was in Redding the past summer. He appeared in a book catalog sent to the home where I was staying, and in a mask made by another friend in his men's group. He followed me in my journey back south, dancing among the trees of Yosemite, playing hide and seek at VisionPoint, weaving his way in and out of conversations with friends. Now in Tucson, he laughs with the Saguaro Cactus guardians of this sacred high desert and plays tricks with coyote. Whenever, wherever, I feel his Presence, every cell of my body tingles with aliveness. This archetype always reappears when humanity needs to be reminded of its right relationship with Nature and I am most grateful for his presence.

The desire to *know* him, to merge with him, intensified. On a busy day in town, the White Buffalo insisted that I turn around and go back to Rainbow Moods, a bookstore I had driven past. There a single copy of the book *GREEN MAN: The Archetype of our Oneness with the Earth* waited for me. The vibrantly, leafy Green Man image on the cover seared itself into my consciousness and the sought merger took place. The sought *knowing* became intuitive. The book, though consciously written, is too left-brained for me. I read the ending first and absorbed the pictures. From time-to-time, I read a page here, a page there. It became an altar object, propped up, full face, braced by a small VisionPoint rock, and companioned by a view-from-space image of Gaia.

The GREEN MAN book sparked my interest in other books about the Male Mysteries. Green Man was reborn in each of them as a fascinating archetype who renews our lost unity with the natural world. This living masculine face of Earth, symbolizing the rebirth of plant life, wooed me. I felt vibrantly alive, loved and erotically revitalized. I was suddenly captivated by the magical desert landscape and its vivid and varied hues of green. Every cell of my body was permeated with Green Man's healing essence as he re-emerged out of the deep past and filled my now with his life affirming presence.

Symbols of Green Man and Gaia had found their way into a simple altar in my home and in my heart. I now gratefully knew that the temple would be The Temple of Gaia and Green Man. And in exploring the eternal love story of Isis and Osiris, I discovered that Osiris, Divine Consort of the Goddess Isis, was often called Green Man. This information strengthened my Priestess of the World connection with the Fellowship of Isis.

More than this, I am in love! Green Man has captured my heart the way a man does when he truly loves that which is woman. He is the Fool! He is the Divine Playmate! He knows that, just as mankind exists because of womankind, he exists because of the feminine principle. He is son, lover, and the guardian of the Great Goddess. He is reappearing now to redress imbalances in our attitude toward Nature and to guide, inspire, and energize us to restore balance. He is supremely intelligent and the guardian and revealer of mysteries.

Green Man, this magical devourer and disgorger of foliage, has come into my life at this time to reveal to me the mystery of death and renewal. That is why he persistently began appearing soon after I received my *death* message in Mount Shasta. He is assisting me in embracing psychic death so I do not have to physically die. Green Man, as the intelligence underlying the World of vegetation, is assisting me in fulfilling my pledge to Gaia. At our ordination, each Priestess gave a gift of Self to the aspect of the Goddess she was called to serve. That day, I had written out a pledge, sealed it in an envelope, and placed it on the temple altar that night. Now it was on my altar and it was time to open it and renew my pledge.

June 26, 1991

Beloved Gaia . . .

As your Priestess, I offer you my communication skills – written, verbal, non-verbal – for the Full-fill-ment of Our Highest Co-Creative Destinies. And I offer my body vehicle for regenerative transformation into a Being of Radiant Vitality, Beauty, Joy, Health, Harmony and Balance.

It Is Done And It Is So! Blessed Be!

With Deepest Love and Devotion,
Nicole Christine/Laughing Brooke

Without realizing it at the time, I volunteered for a death experience in order to bring about regenerative transformation! Gaia sent me the Blue Pharaoh of the Egyptian Mysteries and Green Man of the European Folk Mysteries to assist. Preparation to receive their input was set in motion Spring of 1988 through a reading by an empathic who addressed my life-work commitment to humanity. She said I assist others in their sacred journey by "facilitating deep processing" and indicated that my Guides were concerned with the personal imbalance I had created out of this commitment. Guidance now was to review the transcripts of these readings for their current significance.

"Put your mind where Nicole is nourished for Nicole, so you build and strengthen the central core of yourself. This is very important for your balance and health. You have to centralize the magnetic flow on the outside that reflects and returns and facilitates and orchestrates and combines with the project as it is facilitating it. Otherwise you don't have enough bio-energy on the inside of you. That's not good for the health level of the physical body.

"So when you line up to work with the big guns—those guys up there who send in lots of knowledge—one of the things you have to do is magnetize the central core of the body. The Egyptians knew this. They had lots of ways of working with that, but we are just now getting a handle on it. The central core, the central system of the body which is you. It's Linda Lou. It's Nicole. It's the central part of you and has to be nourished and sustained separate from your interactions with others. It's like that at the moment that you die, you are the only thing that passes. And so you are going to nourish that place within that is the center of you that has nothing to do with anyone else.

"Now . . . they want me to use the metaphor of the death a little more. If you go into a meditation and you imagine yourself dying, it's not difficult for you to slide through into that space. What they are wanting you to do is to *live* in that space, not die in that space. To be in that space inside of you and fill it with life for you. Not to take that space and imbue the project or others so quickly. There's a health concern here . . . you know how to release and surrender which is the dying process of transformation . . . not just the physical death, but of letting go of what is out-of-date in the lifetime and moving onto the next. So you move into that place easily.

"You know how to work with transformational experiences externally, but it's a trilogy. To balance those two points, you have to work with this third aspect that they're spending so much time talking about here which is, from my viewpoint, really the filling, the magnetizing of the central core for you in ways that have nothing to do with projects here. It's just Nicole. And Linda Lou . . . Linda Lou's here, too. Linda Lou has a need to be cherished. And this is cherishing the Linda Lou within. Loving and cherishing the Linda Lou within.

"I would sum up this vibration by saying that I think you've learned all your lessons, which doesn't mean enlightenment. It means that you are integrating now. You're integrating. You're finding balance. And what you're finding balance with is the inner and the outer. The outer focus is tremendous here. The inner magnetism is . . . I think there is meditation here, but meditation is not a strong enough activity on your own behalf. This is activity on your own behalf for yourself where you are thinking of no one but Nicole . . . Linda Lou Nicole.

"For example, when taking a walk on the beach, say, 'From here to the bluff, I'm going to think about projects, others. From the bluff to that house, I'm going to think about me.' And feel yourself. Breathe yourself. Talk to Linda Lou on the inside. Remember things about the past. Enjoy your journey into yourself. And then when you get to the house . . . 'Now, I'll think about projects, others, until I get to the next bluff.' So you begin to work with balance. 'Now I'm project, other-oriented. Now I'm Linda Lou Nicole oriented.'

"See, Linda Lou's got a lot of heart in her. Nicole has a tremendous capacity to take the heart energy and orchestrate it, but Linda Lou is the one who keeps the heart energy and nourishes herself. And that's why I use the two names. Nicole hasn't really mastered that one yet. That was Linda Lou's lesson. And so it's come through into the Nicole name because the lesson hasn't been mastered yet." [10]

&

Oh, yes. The pieces were all there. I was getting the lesson and so the pieces were solidifying, crystallizing. The integration, the balancing of the inner and outer was/is taking place. This integration and balancing vividly outpictured on January 18, 1992 - the sixth anniversary of my last marriage. I had gone into that marriage with such deep intentionality to heal the wounds of separation between the masculine and feminine and felt I had failed because this marriage ended in yet another divorce. The redeeming factor was that this relationship deepened my commitment to inner partnership that would manifest outwardly in a partnership society.

At this time I carry on the outer work, balanced by committed inner work, via the Partnership Way movement that is gaining momentum in Tucson. I committed to facilitate a fund raising journaling workshop for the Partnership Way Center on January 18 on the theme *Inner Partnering of the Masculine and Feminine*. Through journal writing and sharing, participants could discover ways to inwardly fuse the complementary energies of the feminine and the masculine, heart and mind, feelings and thoughts, and lead a more holistic life.

Leaving home for the workshop, I realized the association between the workshop date and the anniversary date. I was clearly persisting in fulfilling my commitment to living in a partnership way. Six is the number of renewal and I had done much to renew myself and step forth again in life revitalized.

There had been wonderfully reinforcing, energizing interest in the workshop from the time I voiced my desire to do it. That Saturday morning, twenty-six women and men, fully committed to the process, unknowingly assisted me in my own inner fusion that outpictured the next morning. Exhausted, I had gone to bed early. I awakened at 6:30 a.m., just as the feminine Full Moon was setting in the West and dawn was breaking in the East where the masculine Sun rises. Ecstatic, I wrapped myself in a snugly afghan inside my cozy little adobe and took in both enactments of the Earth drama simultaneously. The perfection and harmony of it all danced in every cell of my being.

Throughout the day, I was in a state of honeymoon bliss! I had not failed. I was succeeding in ways I had not fathomed when I engaged and disengaged in and from my legal marriages. I felt profoundly grateful for each seen and unseen participant in the sacred service we had shared the day before. I was lifted up knowing that as any one of us is lifted up, all life is lifted up with us. We were all succeeding! We were all fusing and transforming! We had simply fallen in consciousness that we might fuse spirit deeper into matter. Now, we, each in our own way, in our own time, were all lifting in consciousness. This truth was sealed in the evening when, simultaneously, the sun set in the West and the moon rose in the East. How good it is to be alive on Planet Earth!

I left my first marriage because my doctor told me that, given my weak lungs, each year I continued to stay in a cold climate was a year off my life. This husband was afraid to start over elsewhere and leave family, friends, and work behind. After a hard winter of illness, I left on my own. An aunt chastised me saying, "It is your cross to bear to stay with your husband no matter what." This was the sister of my mother who had died when she was nineteen of respiratory problems!

Somehow, perhaps by an act of grace, I refused to buy into this mistaken notion of sacrifice. In many ways, my life and the lives of my sons seem wrought with sacrifice because I did not stay, *no matter what*. But at this point in my journey, I feel extremely blessed to know and feel the true meaning of the word *sacrifice: to make sacred*.

All life is sacred and I feel the Great Spirit moving in all things. This is what it means to live and to die consciously. To have no fear of death is knowing the name of the Great Spirit will be on my lips and in my heart when my time on this planet is complete. Everything I do is a sacred ritual. Typing this work. Eating. Sleeping. When I feed the birds, I throw a handful to the Seven Directions: North, East, South, West, Heaven, Earth, Here. When I choose to wear makeup, it is done in the spirit of costuming and play, in the spirit of accenting my eyes in tribute to the All Seeing Beauty of the Goddess.

I am more attentive to the sacredness of my four body vehicles. I am more conscious about developing both sides of my body and brain. I am increasingly more aware of the plane of synchronicity and to the reality that everything is about everything. Actually, I feel turned inside out as though I have gone through some sort of inversion process. The only impulses now powerful enough to warrant active responses are coming from inner space rather than from what I perceive as my outer environment where I have received direction so much of my life.

Gradually, I am becoming more attuned to the sounds and rhythm of nature. The birds, the plants, the rocks, the all of it, bring such a smile to my soul. I use little artificial lighting and daily thank the sun and the moon for their radiance. I feel in accord with the moon cycles, planting new seeds of consciousness at the new moon, nurturing them at the first quarter, harvesting at the full moon, and resting and reflecting as it wanes.

I thank and bless the herb and mineral supplements I take to help my body restore its true blueprint. I charge the water that I drink and bathe in with the violet ray of healing and transmutation. I celebrate the many hues of Creation by wearing lots of colors and living in an Earth-toned, colorful space. I cherish the Silence and inwardly thank barking dogs and noisy neighbors for giving me yet another opportunity to choose inner peace.

And I thank the Great Mother Goddess/Great Father God and Gaia and Green Man for the opportunity to be rebirthed at this sacred moment in Earth's evolution into higher consciousness. I rejoice in the human experience and in the gifts of good and not so good times that we give to one another. I have not always wanted to live. I have even attempted to take my own life. I want to live now. Now that I am truly beginning to taste Life's sweetness. Now that I am feeling more at ease being my True, Authentic Self.

Soon after returning to Tucson, I learned through a variety of sources that I had been moving through my "Chiron Return." This is a major life transit activated about age fifty by the rather newly discovered celestial body Chiron. Chiron, the *wounded healer,* demands that we enter into the depths of our woundedness that we might be reborn into wholeness as the wounded healer.

I tried to resist facing my woundedness. It felt so all encompassing, so overwhelming. It took a message of imminent death to jar me out of a pathetic slow death at the hands of my own unresolved pain. Death challenged me to fully live, to transmute, to become whole. By moving through my pain, I am tuning into the magical qualities of every aspect of existence. Tucson feels so alive! The human comedy drama feels more delightful! My body feels like a Universe in and of itself! The multi-dimensional nature of the Universe feels more awesome, yet very common!

I *trust the process* more. Though I have not yet fully merged my inner and outer realities, I am more at ease in relating to both simultaneously. Near the end of 1991, I woke up as California was falling into the sea of my inner reality. I did not know if that meant I would never return there or that what California life meant to me had returned to the waters of the Great Mother. I felt no need to analyze what I experienced. Simply observe.

Simply note what came up for me. Guidance was to inwardly complete soul contracts I had with people and places there, except for my three-year-old Goddaughter with whom I have a strong inner connection.

VisionPoint remained intact in my inner Earth and it is easy for me to be there and in Tucson, simultaneously. There is still no tangible resolution around co-stewardship of the land, but there is peace. The destiny of VisionPoint and of my work in Tucson are parallel in intent. For the first time, I could see reason to sell my interest in order to have the resources to expand the spirit and teachings of VisionPoint here. When my VisionPoint partner and I are in sacred right relationship with each other, the land, the Great Spirit, this future will reveal itself. Ownership will become a moot point for no one can own the Earth Mother.

≈

And, so . . . how does one close a never ending story? Perhaps with another story within the story. Just prior to ordination, an intriguing series of events led me to temporarily share housing with Cassandra, another Priestess in my class. She is the youngest and I am the oldest, yet we felt a strong affinity between us. The afternoon I moved in, we talked about how significant it felt to be living together at this time. Due to the intensity of the feeling, I lay on my bed to get in touch with what was trying to break through from my subconscious. Soon a familiar memory surfaced. . . .

I was ordained into the Madonna Ministry with Graham and our friend Ruth. She wore a white, ankle-lengthed dress and when I saw her, a past life memory flashed before me. We were running through an underground tunnel with several other Priestesses dressed in white and carrying scrolls under our arms. The Temple was being destroyed by invaders hostile to the teachings of the Goddess and we were fleeing with as many recorded mysteries as we each could carry. The inner movie always froze at a frame in which Ruth was running just ahead of me on my right and another Priestess I could not identify was running close to me on my left. I had not been able to fast forward that frame no matter how many times I went back to it in consciousness.

As I lay on the bed, the inner reel rolled forward. Cassandra was the other Priestess! The reel could not move until this moment when it was time to remember. Time to remember that as the three of us ran, we vowed that the teachings would not be lost. We encoded the contents of each scroll we carried into our genetic codes to be brought forth at a time when it was again safe for the Goddess to return. We had not known how many, many, many lifetimes we would have to reincarnate in one disguise after another before we could come forward again as Priestesses and live the teachings, live the Great Mystery. That time is now! At last, that time is now! At last! At last!

Printed in the scrolls I carried, encoded in my consciousness, is the teaching that we are, each and everyone of us, Priest and Priestess to the

World . . . and that there will come a time when the World again becomes the temple and there will be no intermediaries for anyone between Heaven and Earth. This will soon be followed by yet another re-awakening. Encoded in the RNA-DNA genetic code of each of us, is the memory of our own Divinity as Sons and Daughters of our Mother Goddess/Father God. In the not so distant future, we will again walk the Sacred Earth as Gods and Goddesses, as the new Archetypes of the New Earth in the ever unfolding, sacred story of Creation. We will know the Great Mystery in the only way It can be known . . . BY LIVING IT, BY BEING IT!

The Work, The Play,
The Blueprint
~As perceived in January 1992~

*T*he work, the play, the blueprint! A Temple of Gaia and Green Man! An Earth Song Institute and Shop! Will this really come to be? What a challenge! Where will the resources come from? Where is the site itself? Or the people to participate? Where is the theater and cast for this script? Do I have the energy and willingness to take on something of this magnitude? Fortunately, there is a gentle dialogue going on inside me and answers to my questions come easily. When I listen, I feel less intimidated by this seemingly monumental undertaking.

Work I truly love always feels like play and I would truly love to do this. If I do not sabotage myself, the blueprint, so perfectly crystalized in the etheric realm, will organically evolve in this physical realm. All will take shape in ways right for the time, place and people involved. [11] I chose this lifetime to manifest a blueprint already divinely designed, and not following through would be more difficult than actualizing what I came here to do. And recently, in updating my resume, I realized my lifetime work in the World has well prepared me for this endeavor.

I am awed by the perfection of it all. Yet, I waver between feelings of excitement and thoughts of absurdity. My White Buffalo takes me down new roads to explore potential sites. When I find a place with promise, I feel this is all really going to happen. However, something always indicates that this is not *it*. I thank the place for helping me energize the blueprint in my consciousness. Then on the way home, I feel stymied by economical and personal *practicalities*. I start thinking what I have written is totally out of touch with *reality*.

But the writing is my primary means of anchoring the blueprint and thoughtform of Priests and Priestesses to the World. By using discretion in sharing the concept with appropriate others, the ideas are energized further which is a manifestation prerequisite. Stay aligned with spirit and the process. Keep heart and mind open. Be *actively receptive* rather than in active pursuit. Everything will unfold according to divine timing and plan. My work now is to hold this perspective and record my present understandings of the blueprint, knowing everything will evolve and change as I evolve and change.

Earth Song Shop

The concept of the shop generates the most apprehension. This is the *in the world* business part of the plan. It is an immediate avenue for income and visibility. A first step toward establishing the larger plan. But, more than that, it is a very personal challenge to integrate my feminine ideals and values with my masculine designs and propensity for action. It is a marriage partnership of giving and receiving, being and doing, love and money. And it is scary! As I explore the possibilities of starting a business, I gain greater insight into myself and my unresolved issues. Money matters are at the core of each issue. I need to heal my personal prosperity consciousness and come to terms with this culture's consumer consciousness. I live simply, yet feel I consume too many of Mother Earth's resources. This puts me at odds with the idea of owning a shop and the corresponding need to attract customers.

I look at money as green energy and the current means of exchange, but have not made peace with the mainstream preoccupation with owning things, things, things! Possessed by possessions. Separation from nature. The social norm. My inner ecologist is easily outraged. She is not impressed with bandaide campaigns such as recycling. She wants to get to the root cause of conspicuous consumption. Recently, she got into a huff hearing a friend comment that the healing effect of flower essences was similar to sitting in a field of flowers. My inner ecologist asserted, *See! If people would just live closer to nature, we would not need to bottle up the essences of flowers!*

My inner healer penetrated my cloud of indignation to state, *Neither you nor many others in this country know how to live close to nature. The flowers are giving their essences to be bottled to help humanity heal the separation. Honor their gifts, Nicole. Honor their gifts.*

Each time I get into a similar huff about becoming a shop owner, that same sweet Voice gently encourages me to consider the possibility that conscious consumption can trigger a *reverse mode*. This could help us find our way back Home. A shop with *Earth-Honoring* creations could serve Gaia by calling our attention back to Nature and forward to fuller recognition of our creative talents. So, slowly, I open to the possibility that this aspect of the work could raise the consciousness of our right relationship to Earth, Nature, and one another.

The shop will carry books, art, musical cassette tapes, and healthy planet products. Books will include those that express a New Earth consciousness and, eventually, writings authored and published by Priests and Priestesses honoring Celestial Earth as the Sacred Temple. Other merchandise will include Sonoran Desert herbs, seeds, and flower essences and music, jewelry, and art that reflect Earth-Centered spirituality and the multi-cultural, multi-racial diversity of greater Tucson. Most merchandise will be acquired within the Sonoran Desert bio-region. However, local, global, and cosmic consciousness will be reflected overall. Inventory focusing on Gaia, Green Man, the White Buffalo, and White Buffalo Calf Woman will be featured items. The shop will also serve as an ecological information and resource center with particular emphasis on bio-regionalism and the buffalo restoration movement. Sound ecological practices will be consistently implemented and re-evaluated in running the shop.

Earth Song Institute

In the beginning, initiatory training will be one-to-one until a full-fledged program is established. As more Priest-ess Initiates come forth, the shop will serve as a gathering place. The institute will always remain small enough to ensure intensive, individualized training. This will ensure that what develops is built on the knowledge, experience and personal truth of each participant and facilitates manifestation of their own blueprints. Initially, I will serve as facilitating coordinator to focalize development. Eventually, a coordinating council of six Priests and six Priestesses will evolve. Decision-making will be based on a partnership consensus model.

Earth Song Institute (ESI) Program goals include:
- finding and expressing one's True Voice
- rebirthing and naming the Authentic Self
- seeing and experiencing multi-dimensionality and the relatedness of all aspects of one's life to all other aspects of Life
- exploring individual and shared creativity that moves us into co-creative expression with Nature and the Creator/Creatrix
- developing a community system of organization that interweaves bio-regional, multi-racial culture, politics, economics, art, spirituality and ecology
- enhancing communication skills by learning to talk more effectively and less often, and to intently listen within and without

Rituals and ceremonies will be integral components of institute activities. Priestesses will keep New Moon Lodges and develop appropriate contemporary rites of passage for women. Priests will actualize activities appropriate for men and co-create Green Man activities. Men and women will participate in Full Moon and other community celebrations and rituals. Ordination candidates will co-create their ordination rite with one another, myself, Gaia and Green Man.

Curriculum Program

Training will be based on the human nine month birthing cycle beginning at the Autumn Equinox and completing near Summer Solstice. The intensity of the curriculum will maximize a quantum leap in consciousness that will assist each Initiate in actualizing their Sacred Work as a Priest or Priestess to the World. Programming will always be individualized to encompass each ordination candidate's worldly life.

There will be one three-hour group session per week facilitated by a staff person. A semimonthly group session will be co-created by participants and be a time for music, art, dance, discussion, and drama. Every other week, a two hour private session will be arranged with me or another staff member to focus on individual needs. Individuals may choose to supplement their course work through involvement in related activities offered in the larger community. Each Initiate will be asked to contribute to the ongoing care of the Temple and Institute grounds and buildings.

The keeping of a personal journal will be a primary requirement of the program, but no one need share any part of it if they choose to keep their writings private. This will facilitate integration and documentation of this cosmically significant period of transformation. Utilization of personal, planetary, and galactic knowledge available through Medicine Wheel Earth Astrology and Zodiacal Astrology will be encouraged. Recommended readings, writing projects, and self-evaluation methods will be suggested, but each person will be free to determine the resources and evaluation tools most appropriate to their personal growth. Emphasis will always be on encouraging participants to go within for guidance and to do only that which they resonate with as true for them.

First Trimester: Know YourSelf

The focus will be on increased awareness of one's physical, emotional, mental and spiritual nature. Individuals will be assisted in identifying how to further such awareness beyond the scope of what ESI programming offers. For example, one might better know one's physical self by developing an improved health care program and receiving appropriate input from other sources. Participation in a co-dependency group or in a support group focused on feeling feelings might further the knowing of one's emotional self. A course in astrology, numerology, or mythology could stimulate mental self-awareness, while dance, movement or drumming classes could enhance spiritual, physical, emotional, and mental awareness. Each Initiate will be fully supported in maintaining any other spiritual or religious affiliation they may choose.

Core programming will include the inner fusion of the right and left sides of the brain, the feminine and masculine energies, and the realms of feeling and thought. The relationship of sensuality, eroticism, sexuality, and spirituality will be discriminately explored as part of the process of self-definition. Breath work to assist us in again "breathing with the Creator" and other processes for total integration of all aspects of self will be ongoing facets of the training. Tears, laughter, and demonstrations of mutual love and respect will facilitate the process.

Second Trimester: Know Nature as YourSelf

This three month period will focus on attuning to the qualities and patterns found in nature and in ourselves. We will co-discover what the plants, rocks, trees, and creatures that inhabit Earth Song Institute grounds are here to give and receive in their life journeys. We will open to discover more about ourselves through Nature that we might remember we are each parts of a shared Whole. Attunement to the greater Tucson area will be encouraged via group outings and individual involvement in other nature activities widely available in this area. This overall process will enhance our abilities to harmonize with Earth's song.

Third Trimester: The Sacred Dance of Co-Creation, Celebration, and Ritual

Now emphasis will be on co-creating rituals and ceremonies so we may reassume our place in creation in ways that are dynamic, creative, responsive, and at one with All That Is. Exploration of indigenous, pagan, eastern and western traditions will be encouraged, but the primary focus will be on inner directed co-creation of rituals and ceremonies relevant to these times. Celebration of our connection with Gaia and Green Man and rhythmic participation in the Sacred Dance of co-creation and rebirth will be an on-going facet of the ESI experience.

The Temple And The Site

The Temple/Institute site already actively exists in the etheric realms above Tucson. There are many variations in the ways it will manifest in the physical realm. The one I favor outpictures on several acres outside Tucson. It is essential for Priestesses and Priests to the World, for humanity itself, to "re-land our consciousness,"[12] to firmly establish sacred relationships with Gaia and Green Man, Earth and Nature.

It seems likely that raw land would be obtained first. And, at last, the yurt I keep seeing myself in will have a land base. This circular, canvas structure would serve as a temporary shelter and ceremonial hut. Whatever occurs on any site, in any structure, will be done in harmony with the sacred truth of the place and space. Resources needed to build appropriate structures will become available through the power of clear intent and pragmatic clarity. I see potential for several adobe and earthburmed structures on the grounds. However, at this time, I am only addressing my inner vision of the central adobe structure to house the temple, the institute and me.

The Inner Temple of Gaia and Green Man

The inner temple will be the heart space of the structure with easy access to the outer temple, Earth. I see light pouring through windows and walls colorfully painted and accented in Earth tones. The floor is tiled and the room furnished simply, comfortably, naturally. There is a large fireplace and hearth that makes up the altar. On this wall is a large mural of the sun and a man on one side of the fireplace and the moon and a woman on the other side. The man and woman are holding up the Earth painted above the center of the fireplace. The mural depicts the external beauty and balance we create through inner harmony between our masculine and feminine aspects.

To strengthen conscious awareness that all life is sacred and thus all that we do is sacred, the inner temple will be a multi-purpose space for rituals, ceremonies, meditation, classes, and group interactions. It will be a space where we deepen our awareness of our divinity and our holy relationship to one another, Earth, Nature, Life Itself. A space in which we actualize our co-creative roles in the ever evolving story of Creation.

Remaining Rooms

The remaining space will consist of a library/study, conference room, office, community kitchen, guest room, bathrooms and a living/bedroom for me.

The Grounds

I yearn for the day when I can give attention to co-creating with nature on land where the natural landscape is honored and enhanced with butterfly, hummingbird, moon, herb, and vegetable gardens. At all times, people present on the land will be encouraged to show deep respect and appreciation for it and to develop sacred relationships with the rocks, plants, and creatures who make their home there.

Whenever feasible, rituals and ceremonies will be held outdoors. At times, complete Silence will be the most appropriate way to be with the land. Other times, lively, festively noisy activities will be more fitting. My favorite vision is of a garden full of people laughing, singing, and dancing around a central flag pole where a raised Earth Flag gloriously flies in the wind. My heart sings joyfully at this sight.

And at the entrance to the land, I see an adobe wall that borders the roadway. It was hand built by Priestesses of Gaia and Priests of Green Man. The wall is painted with a life-size mural of a black buffalo herd and the White Buffalo and White Buffalo Calf Woman. These words from the *Gaia Matrix Oracle*[13] are prominently inscribed on the wall to inspire all who pass our way. . .

WHEN THE BUFFALO RETURN FREELY
TO THE FACE OF THE EARTH
THIS WILL BE A SIGN
OF THE COLLECTIVE BEGINNING
OF THE PERIOD "TO MAKE SACRED."
THIS SACRIFICE STAGE IS INITIATED BY
THE WHITE BUFFALO ARCHETYPE
OF COMPLETE ESSENCE
WHEN ONE IS ON THE PATH OF
REVELATION AND TRUTH.

The Next Step

~January 28, 1992~

*A*s I reached completion in writing *The Work, The Play, The Blueprint,* a great tide of emotion swelled up within me. I realized that all I had written exists in my inner Earth. An enormous wave of freedom, humility, gratitude, and joy moved through me, washing away my economical and emotional misgivings. Doubts were drowned by an undertow of words. . .

Turn it over . . . turn it over . . . turn it over . . .

Turn it over to the Great Mother from whence it came. Place your writing on the altar as your gift to Her when you are ordained as a High Priestess, a Crystal Priestess to Gaia. Then let go . . . let go . . . let go. Allow for the period of gestation needed on the physical plane. Do not get stuck in the quagmire of expectations and plans. Do more than trust the process. BE THE PROCESS! Stay clear! Know your Self. All will unfold in divine perfection. Nothing more. Nothing less.

IT IS DONE AND IT IS SO IN THE SACRED NAME
OF THE GREAT MOTHER. BLESSED BE!

Part Two

The Process
~As reflected upon in early 1995~

*T*ruly trusting the process is empowering. I travel within a wonderful labyrinth of processes within processes - an intricate maze that is becoming less difficult and more adventurous. The very writing of this work is filled with processes within the writing process. The first draft of The Temple of Gaia and Green Man was completed on January 27, 1992. Now, three years later, *The Temple of The Living Earth* rewrite bears testimony to a transformative process. As I refine and update, I am aware that I am spiraling in consciousness, making new passes over old ground from a perspective of higher consciousness. I now see and celebrate how The Process of my Sacred Work/Play is evolving. I trust the Creative Process.

My Sacred Sisters, Maya and Bridget, reviewed and edited the draft for me. In so doing, they awakened their Inner Priestess. Even before I had the final manuscript mailed to The Fellowship of Isis in Ireland, they committed to becoming Priestesses to the World. By late February of 1992, their initiatory process was in motion.

On Valentine's Day, my son Todd and I discovered the location destined to become Earth Song Institute and Shop. Four days later, without knowing how I would finance the undertaking, I paid the rental deposit and signed a one year lease. I arrived home and found a letter from the escrow company that handled the trust deed on a divorce settlement property. The borrowers had refinanced and would be paying me off in two weeks! This meant a substantial loss in long term interest payments, but was confirmation that the blueprint fully intended to manifest now.

My sons enthusiastically pitched in to help me set up shop in the one hundred year old commercialized duplex in the Fourth Avenue business district. The money arrived from escrow and quickly went back out in the world as Todd and I shopped for fixtures, supplies, and merchandise. Knowing my disdain for consumerism, he asked how I felt about spending so much money. I laughed and replied, "I have no idea if I can make a go of this, but I'm sure gonna have fun trying!" Todd approaches shopping with zeal and we did, indeed, have fun. Joel helped me select and set up stereo, television, and video equipment. He lived nearby and often dropped in to say hello. I loved this new context for our relationships.

I was enthusiastically supported by friends. All external signs were affirming. Inner guidance kept me at ease. I was *in the flow*. When I found myself efforting, I realigned with the blueprint intention. Dealings with the city about signage for the historical building and the landlord about improvements repeatedly knocked me out of alignment. Yet, in a few magical weeks, an attractively displayed two room shop with a cozy temple/group room appeared!

An invitational Earth Song Open House was held Earth Day, April 22, 1992. Over fifty friends participated in the celebration, bringing gifts of greenery, flowering beauty, and basketry. An Earth Flag was raised on a pole in the front yard. An island of the planet was reclaimed for Earth Mother in the sea of the city. I proclaimed. . .

> *I pledge allegiance to the Earth*
> *One Planet, One People*
> *Individuated and Whole*
> *Living in Peace and Divine Harmony*
> *With Nature*
> *One Another*
> *And All That Is. Aho.*

Back inside, everyone gathered in the front room. I dedicated Earth Song to Gaia and read the international Earth Day Prayer. Next came the unveiling of the "Inner Partnering" oil painting pictured on the cover of this book. It hung over the fireplace as a harbinger of the wall mural that will be painted on the fireplace wall of the yet to manifest Inner Temple of Gaia and Green Man. I had commissioned visionary artist Sharon Nichols, and she beautifully portrayed my inner landscape of partnership with the planet and the masculine and feminine. The evening ended with music by visionary singer and White Buffalo Calf Woman sister, Cynthia Stacey. Earth Song was celebrated and sung alive. The seeds were sown!

Earth Song opened for business two days later on April 24. I now began my learn-as-you-go crash course in marketing and self-management. I still resisted retailing and wanted to simply run a center. However, it was obvious that people were more apt to come in to explore a store than a center. Invariably, inquiries about merchandise led to animated discussions about our relationship to the Earth. This I loved, but this did not tally up in lucrative ways at closing time each day.

What did begin to nurture me and pay the rent were Earth Song Institute activities. Sixty people gathered in the yard under the June Full Moon and performed Dance to Mend the Sacred Hoop. This Dance was performed by smaller groups for thirteen evenings in July to anchor the "Time Shift" marked by the Mayan Calendar. In the fall, more people gathered for a Full Moon Prayer and Talking Circle for the Freedom of Oglala Sioux Leonard Peltier and Our Planet.

Monthly journaling groups formed, and my individual journal writing sessions increased. New Moon Lodge ceremonies occurred for women. Men and women were invited to Full Moon gatherings. Dream Circles, ritual workshops, and video showings were routine. I developed an Earth Song newsletter to publicize the events and generate Earth Honoring awareness. And by autumn, I was exhausted! I routinely came in by 9:30 a.m. to open the shop and worked on through evening activities. Often, I did not return to my cozy desert adobe home before midnight.

But I never closed the shop at night without having learned more about myself and life. Often the cameo experiences were the most profound. Many "Save the Earth" proponents came in with wholesale products to sell or literature they wanted distributed. One afternoon, I was visited by a young man marketing endangered species T-shirts. He enthusiastically declared that, due to special treatment of the dyes, the animals disappeared when the wearer went outside. He invited me outdoors with him to see the wolf on his shirt disappear. We went out and the wolf did, indeed, disappear. He was pleased with the statement the shirts made and wanted to hear my impression. I felt extreme sadness that provided me with new insight. I replied, "Earth Song exists to bring back the spirit of the wolf, not to focus on its disappearance."

We went back inside where I showed him the beautiful wolf images I carried. "I spent nearly twenty years of my life as a political activist and I'm glad I did. I learned a lot and believe I made some differences. But the biggest lesson was that struggling against something makes it real, and the more I reacted politically to external forces, the more I empowered the struggle. I support you in what you are doing, but, at this time in my life, I believe I can do more to bring back the wolf by energizing its presence rather than its disappearance." I do not believe my words were understood, but I was now clearer about my new phase of Earth advocacy.

People were drawn to the spirit of the wolf and related pictures, posters, calendars, and books sold well. Retail sales were improving and the modestly priced Institute fees were a consistent source of income, but I could not afford employees. All my working life I felt overworked and underpaid by my employers. Now I was my own employer, and was working harder and longer without pay. Friends volunteered to relieve me, but this did not lighten the load. Earth Song Institute was already outgrowing the group

room, and soon nights would be too cold for outdoor activities. Synchronistically, the adjacent guest house, adorned with Green Man ivy, became
available for rent. A spiritual sister committed to cover the rent for six
months. Earth Song Institute moved into Raven House. Women gathered to
form a Women's Lodge Council. Larger indoor activities took place. Movement. Creative Expression workshops. Mask and drum making events. Poetry
readings. Storytelling.

This Priestess of Gaia felt like an indentured servant to the World! Was
this BEING THE *PROCESS*? Why then, was my life overrun with *doingness*?

Nonetheless, I was expanding in consciousness by this mergance of the
spiritual and material worlds. The shop became a natural setting for spiritually centered interactions. An interesting variety of people hung out because
the shop "felt so good." Hesitantly, I followed Guidance to add D.D. to my
name on the Earth Song business card. This felt ostentatious and misrepre-
sentative of the award given *Doctors of Divinity* within the patriarchal religious
system. But these two letters often led to discussions of Gaian Spirituality.
When asked about the significance of the letters, I would smile and say, "I
am a *Daughter of Divinity*." Sometimes, I even talked about the intensive
spiritual training I receive on the Inner Realms and found that my inquirers
were quite interested.

My Doctoral Certificate had arrived from Ireland on March 26. Lady
Olivia lovingly commended the paper and my commitment. I was bursting
with joy! This meant more to me than any academic treatise I had ever seen
or done. The Certificate was the Sacred Seal on my Scriptural Scroll.

A month later I was again honored by Lady Olivia. She sent another
certificate in response to my request to have Earth Song identified as a
Fellowship of Isis Temple and School. Acknowledging my dedicated response to the *Call of the Goddess*, she also certified me as a Priestess Hierophant. Though this news arrived after Earth Song was opened, her actions
were dated April 23, 1992 — the date between the Earth Day Open House
and the shop opening. I was living on a divine time line.

Maya and Bridget were the only Priestess Initiates. We followed the
curriculum guidelines described in the doctoral dissertation, but their Priestess process was largely separate from the daily Earth Song process. Institute
activities had taken on a life of their own. Rather than implementing an
Institute or Fellowship of Isis curriculum, I often co-ordinated events facilitated by a diverse representation of Tucson's spiritually gifted women.

I did explore obtaining religious non-profit status for Earth Song. This
process helped me see that the Goddess could not, would not, be restricted
to the narrow confines of governmental regulations. But my efforts were not
wasted. While trying to draw up bylaws, I tapped into the *Guiding Principles
of Earth/Gaian Centered Spirituality* and to the thoughtform of the planet as
The Temple of the Living Earth. Thus I became more conscious of the new
paradigm I am moving into.

My first *official* act as a Hierophant was to perform the marital Rite of

Hieros Gamos for Lady Elena and Lord Kenneth. This was a very celebratory event and I felt honored to bless their union in the Name of the Goddess. The morning of the marriage, I awakened to memories of lifetimes, after the Goddess was banned, in which this wedding party performed this Rite. Often risking our lives, we performed this ceremonial lifting up of a Higher Love to benefit all Life. We did so in groves, dungeons, caves, and open meadows. We did so to insure that the ways of the Goddess would never die.

We had contracted to do this until it was safe for the Goddess to re-emerge. The time was now. The completion of this ceremony fulfilled our contract. I shared my recall with the wedding party, triggering memories for others. I knew when this day was over, we would journey apart. The Goddess wanted to express in new ways.

❧

I, too wanted to express in new ways! No matter how I rationalized the advantages of having a shop, I *hated* retailing more each day. I wanted to re-negotiate my contract with Gaia at whatever levels I had made it. Yet, I knew my intense negative reaction to sales represented something that needed healing within me. My stress level mounted. Driving home after a particularly long day, I called out to the stars. "What is it I'm not getting? I want to get the lesson now!"

I dropped into bed without undressing and fell right to sleep. I woke up screaming and bolted upright. My scream intensified, rising up from the bowels of my being. It scared me, but I could not stop it. Suddenly, I was in the first enclosed shopping mall in the small Wisconsin town I had lived in during the late sixties. Joel, age three, was with me as I hurried past one openly exposed store after another in search of a stationery store. Back then, I did not realize I was having a panic attack. While making my purchases, I hit sensory overload. I held back the scream, but not my urge to run. Grabbing my package in one hand, and Joel's little hand in my other, I dragged him along. Soon both of us were crying. I did not stop until we reached our car.

The Voice of the Inner Comforter spoke. Alone in the desert, twenty-five years and thousands of miles away, I heard what I could not hear then. *Turn around. Look.* Still screaming, I turned around. A tidal wave of consumerism was crashing down on us. I screamed louder and started to run again. *Stop. Let it crash. You are safe. So is Joel.* I stopped. The wave crashed. We did not drown. We were safe. *Where there's no resistance, there's no harm.*

I had ridden the crest of that wave as a teenager employed in one of the town's first supermarkets. It was fun to work in that shiny, streamlined store that encouraged Mom and Pop corner store friendliness. But now, the corner stores were mall parking lots and shopping for mass produced products was an addiction. Exhausted, I lay back down and cried myself to sleep. I could finally stop running.

When I awakened in the morning, I knew I had reclaimed the fragmented part of myself that could not comprehend the worldly takeover of trinkets and things. Emotionally traumatized by this sudden shift in my reality, an aspect of who I had been before the invasion had splintered off and ran and ran and ran. It felt strangely as if the shop existed just to force me to face my fear and, having done so, I could move on to something else. The crashing wave washed away my hatred. All I felt was exhaustion. I was tired. Very, very tired. How I wanted the Mayan Time Shift to be real! How I wanted to experience the transformational spiral from three-dimensional, mechanistic "time is money" consciousness to fourth dimensional "time is art" natural planetary consciousness. How I wanted to co-create individual and shared destinies and a New Earth wherein art, not money, is the medium of exchange. I wanted my very life to be an art form!

Instead, I was experiencing an emotional and physical downward spiral. In seeking health care alternatives, I bought into the excesses of purging the body of impurities. Early in summer, I began a seven-day cleanse in which I only ingested natural concoctions guaranteed to rid my body of any parasites or toxins lurking within. In five days, I lost seven pounds and most of my energy. On the fifth night I fell into a restless sleep before nightfall. I was awakened by a loud inner message. *Stop starving yourself! You're traumatizing your nervous system. You are not impure. You need nurture! Feed your body and your soul.*

My body trembled as I timidly offered it broth. Was this the great new world wherein I starved and overworked myself? I promised to eat well, then broke the promise daily by being caught up in *time is money* consciousness and forgetting food. After six months as a shopkeeper, I often felt too exhausted to eat. The exhaustion felt greater than the result of this work or even of a lifetime of work. Oh, I was tired. I needed rest. Something had to change.

さ

My relationship with VisionPoint and with Graham had slipped into limbo, but we communicated occasionally. He sent me the chapter "First & Second Wave" from the book *The Star-Borne*. Too busy to read it when it arrived, I put the writing aside. Now the pages called to me.

"Some of the First Wave arrived after the descent into matter, bringing with them many useful talents and skills to aid humanity through its long passage towards reawakening. They have served here with dedication. Their experiences have been arduous and their sacrifices great. For much of their lengthy cycle of service, they have labored under the illusion of being here alone and cut off from Source. The weight of their responsibility has been a heavy burden indeed for these very old souls." [14]

I sobbed in resonance with the words and from the weight of habitually shouldering responsibility even when it did not serve to do so. Graham identified me as First Wave and himself as Second, recognizing how these different origins had generated conflict between us. "The Second Wave entered this planet after it was created and the etheric blueprint set into position." [15] They had a much shorter cycle of Earthly embodiments and thus less experience than those of the First Wave. They are the builders and manifestors of the New Earth and are riddled with impatience to create new forms. They are not concerned with the First Wave responsibility of anchoring energies.

"Unfortunately, there cannot be full expression of their creative potential until Earth's transformation is achieved. This is why it is imperative for First & Second Wave beings to work together at this time. Many of the First Wave are weary, having experienced such a prolonged immersion into the third dimension density. They need the help of the fresh energy and optimism of the Second Wave in order to fulfill their cycle of service.

"It is imperative for the Second Wave to wake up quickly. The very pinions of this planet are being replaced. It's like a changing of the guard, and you are the ones to take the place of First Wave beings who depart. A scepter is being passed, and if you are not in position to take it, who will be?" [16]

I closed shop long enough to go purchase this book by Solara. I returned to Earth Song, but did not reopen for business. Instead, I curled up in the temple room and absorbed the book until I reached "The Quantum Leap" chapter. I trembled and sobbed as I read and remembered this story of Creation. *The Star-Borne. The Angels. The Fall. The Golden Cord. The Call.*

And as the story ended, I sighed. Now I could rest.

You have done your work here well,
Dear Servers of Divine Destiny,
By transmuting the density
Into ever higher octaves
Of accelerated vibrations of Light
You have hereby entered upon
The accelerated path homeward. [17]

That night I slept better than I had in nine months since I began writing my dissertation and anchoring the energies of the Gaia and Green Man matrix. I awakened refreshed and lucid, knowing how crazy it might look to others if I followed the course revealing itself me. During the next few days, I spoke with many of the First Wave, identifiable by their level of fatigue. Many cried as I told the story. Some rejected it as "more New Age woo woo." I made a list of people I recognized as Second Wave. The name Malena Marshall stood out from the rest.

Early in October, I was leaving for Greece to participate in the International Partnership Way Conference on Crete. I would be gone three weeks and wavered between closing the shop or training someone to take over for me. Third-dimensionally, it made more sense to close rather than train and pay someone more than she was likely to sell. Cosmically, I realized that more was at play. It was time to pass the scepter and Malena was the symbolic Second Wave recipient. I did not know what she would think of the Star-Borne information. However, I did know that this sister loved the Earth and Earth Song.

Malena welcomed the opportunity to work at Earth Song. I sensed I would either leave the planet in Greece or be so transformed by the trip that I could not return to life as I knew it. Once again, Guidance was to get my affairs in order. I was to will Earth Song to Malena if she was agreeable to receive it. She could run it or sell it. She agreed.

Late September, knowing I risked my credibility, I shared the Star-Borne Creation Story with the forming women's council gathered at Raven House. Presenting the story as one of many ways to perceive Creation, I spoke of the First and Second Waves. I spoke of the fatigue. The exhaustion. The need for the Changing of the Guard. Of my readiness to leave the planet for R&R. Of the sense I might not return from Greece. Then I symbolically passed the scepter by ritualistically giving Malena a set of keys to Earth Song. She accepted with a willing heart.

The women present responded in emotionally diverse ways. Resonance. Tears. Fear. Support. Anger. Hostility. Accusations of betrayal. Excitement. Resistance. Joy. Release. All expressed in one room in one hour. By the New Moon, it was over and done.

ঽ৶

In the aftermath, I wondered what I had been thinking to say and do what I did. I wondered what the women were thinking and saying. But there was no time to find out. I had to train Malena. Draw up a new Will & Testament. Get out the next newsletter. Even though there was little in it to foretell the turning of the wheel, it felt more like a eulogy than a pronouncement of ongoing events.

I gave my sons new copies of my Will, *just in case*. I did not sing them another of my "Feel like I'm Gonna Die" songs. What was going on with me?!

I *responsibly* got everything at home and at Earth Song in the best possible order. I cleaned, organized, wrote lists and letters. I finished packing for Greece at 2:00 a.m. the morning of my departure. I slept until 4:00 a.m., then rose to leave for the airport. I had one more thing to do before leaving the country. That was to write a letter to Graham. This was my first opportunity to fully express what I was feeling. My words flowed onto the page all the way from Tucson to Washington, DC. I felt deeply relieved when I dropped the lengthy letter in a mail box at Dulles Airport moments before boarding a plane for Greece.

ঽ৶

Greece was a homecoming! Every bone in my body knew Greece. It had called to me for as long as I could remember in this lifetime. Athens: the Acropolis. Delphi: Athena's Sanctuary, Apollo's Pytherium. Spili: village-made yogurt, honey, and walnuts; old women garbed in black; solemn Priests robed in brown. Matala:

caves where Christians once hid from the Romans and hippies from the capitalists, the Mediterranean Sea where Zeus forcefully brought captive Europa ashore. Volcanic Santorini: Ancient Thera, 7th Century B.C.; temples to Isis and Serapis (Osiris). I had lived and died many times in this part of the world. I knew the ways of these Gods and Goddess and of the patriarchs of Greek Orthodoxy, *re-membering* because of their strange, present day co-existence in the cities and countryside. *Re-membering* . . . bringing together dismembered fragments of my soul lingering in this land.

The Crete conference, itself, held little meaning for me. It was the hook to get me to return on a more personal mission. In ruins away from the tourist flow at Knossos, I heard, *You have returned to reclaim fragmented parts of yourself.* Here the Ancient Priestess from the past met the New Priestess of the present. It was a healing reunion. This was the opportunity that, if taken, would transform my life, move me closer to wholeness. I took it. We merged. I was transformed by reclaiming my ancient sacred lineage.

The Partnership Conference was a production! Partnership, for me, is a process. I found it difficult to align with the academic aspects of the conference and often slipped away to the ocean. My soul hungered to draw on the energies of the Goddess-centered, egalitarian Minoan Culture that permeated this land called Crete. I did the Dance to Mend the Sacred Hoop on the rooftop of the conference center that I might cellularly integrate Heaven and Earth, within and without, the masculine and the feminine. I held the intent to anchor Goddess energies, but realized that the Goddess simply *is*. I simply needed to absorb Her into my being.

I gravitated toward others who sought spiritual communion with one another, the Goddess, the land and sea. We planned our own closing ceremony for the last night. Our numbers grew by word-of-mouth. Nearly a hundred women and men gathered by the sea under the full moon. A workshop facilitator took charge in classic dominator mode. Many of us drifted away. I wandered down the shore to do a closing ritual of my own. I expressed my disappointments to the Great Mother. She replied, *You showed up. That was all that was required of any of you. Each of you made arduous journeys over thousands of years to return again to these shores. Simply by showing up together again in this place, cellular memories were activated. This had to happen before any of you could begin to create anew. This will happen. Be patient and attentive, my Daughter. Thank you, my Priestess. Thank you all.*

That moment fed my spirit. The Greek food fed my body and soul! It was alive with Greek love for life. I gained back much welcomed weight. I loved the slower pace of life and grew rested. But exhaustion quickly reclaimed its hold on me by the time I completed the long journey back to Tucson. I slept all the next day and night, getting up only once to check in with Malena. Things had gone slowly, but well, at Earth Song. She was glad I was back. She did not think she would enjoy being a shop owner either.

The following day, without even leaving my house, I knew life had changed for me. I called another friend and said, "I think I need to sell

Earth Song."

She responded, "I think I'll buy it."

❧

Talk about processes! Glena and I jumped through all sorts of hoops working out a sales agreement. We wanted to find a fair, compassionate way to do business with each other and to deal with our personal financial issues as they emerged. We argued, laughed and cried together. Finally, the price and terms were agreed to as well as a closing sale date. I was taking an economic loss, but I had gained considerable insight through this overall venture. In order to simplify tax matters, we agreed that Earth Song would change hands at midnight December 31, 1992.

I had two more months with Earth Song. Business picked up because I no longer resented it and because Christmas was coming. However, participation in Raven House activities dissipated. I no longer held the focus or the vision. Differences that had seemed insignificant between Raven Sisters, were now sources of friction. I wondered what others were thinking of my seeming loss of commitment to Gaia. I felt I was disappointing the community that had begun growing around Earth Song. Disappointing my sons by again leaving what had become a home base for us. Even disappointing my parents who had visited from the Midwest and liked what they saw.

People who live stationary, outer directed lives tend to perceive me as leading a most unsettled life. I did not know how to communicate the continuity I experience in my ever changing, inner directed world. I, too, questioned my reality; not because it seemed inappropriate, but because I wanted to grasp it more fully.

Two answers came that provided a larger context for my latest shift. The first came through Graham. In response to my letter, he recommended that I read *The Crystal Stair: A Guide to the Ascension*, channeled by Eric Klien. Graham believed I would be "ascending" soon and that this material would help me consciously prepare.

I consumed this book. I could not fully embrace it, but the material clearly activated higher levels of my consciousness. A bigger question arose. Why the Call to serve Gaia and the Call to ascend? I decided to find the answer by arranging to meet the publisher in the near future.

In the meantime, I continued to begin each day at Earth Song as I had from the start. I raised the Earth Flag and reaffirmed my commitment to our Earth Mother. Then I stood in the open doorway and telepathically called to all who could benefit by coming to Earth Song that day. Invariably, people yearning to heal their separation from Earth visited. They passed through the doorway, an activation portal for New Earth energies, often without knowing why they came. Something always shifted for me and for them by their coming. When they left, many tied a brightly colored ribbon on the Prayer Fence that bordered the front lawn.

The number of such visitors increased as my time in the shop decreased. People felt compelled to come by; some even said they received Guidance to *See Nicole*. Spiritual discussions ensued and even talk of ascension. During these interactions, no one else entered the portal until we were complete. This was great for the soul; not so great for business. The question of how to function on the planet while being pulled into ascension energies kept coming up for them and for me.

I had felt I was leaving the planet for nearly a decade. What if I was just in some crazy death and rebirth cycle? Had Earth Song been a trial run? Would I stay on the planet to co-create the larger vision at a later time? If I had broken ground and sown seeds, growth had better organically involve others! I was not going to hang around to work as hard as I had this year on my own.

And what did being a Priestess in the 1990s have to do with any of this? Bridget and Maya ceremonially became self-proclaimed Priestesses of Gaia at the Winter Solstice. When we engaged that vibrational field, it felt more real to us than anything else in our lives. When we were outside that field, Priestessing did not seem to have much to do with anything. The harmonics of higher consciousness were vibrantly at play in the spiritual, etheric realm while the forces of the collective consciousness in the material, physical realm felt dull and stifling. Why was it so hard to bridge dimensions? To harmonize vibrational fields?

The second answer regarding my latest shift came on December 26. It was my birthday and I gifted myself with an astrological reading. There were strong indications that 1993 would not be a lucrative year for me to be in business or to accomplish any substantial objectives. I welcomed this confirmation of my need to sell Earth Song. Resting, relaxing, traveling in the White Buffalo as I planned, would be the best way to get through the upcoming "zombie period." I committed to embrace this period as a time for rest and renewal.

Given my propensity to leave everything brighter, shinier, and more orderly than I found it, I was cleaning and organizing Earth Song until nearly midnight on December 31. Those last few hours were nostalgic. Earth Song was an enchanting entity, and we had bonded in consciousness. I loved her. She had taught me things about myself I had been unable to perceive. She had welcomed many of Earth's children wanting to return Home to the Mother. I was both sad and relieved to close and lock the door for the last time.

&

At noon New Year's Day, I also said good-bye to my little adobe sanctuary. It had been a nurturing space to come home to after long hours at Earth Song. It, too, cleanly sparkled and would be an inviting haven for the next resident. What I did not need for travel was stored at Raven House. It was easy for me to pick up and go. Not so easy to stop and rest. This new year I was changing that pattern. By nightfall, I would check into a comfortable, funky resort in Desert Hot Springs, California. Here I would rest in healing waters.

I was delighted by the way I transited from a very active year of doing, doing, doing, into a relatively inactive year of being, being, being. I resolved to learn to live in balance between the two. My zombie year, 1993, was not completely devoid of accomplishments, but I was very content to amble. The irony of having a shop dedicated to the Earth was that I spent most of my time indoors. It was so good to be out and about again. I much preferred being a gypsy than a homebody. True balance and harmony meant flowing with cycles of doing and being, of moving and staying still.

I spent January with friends near VisionPoint as heavy rains made it difficult to get to the land. Then I returned to Tucson for a month to close out Raven House. Glena did not want this space. I was paying the rent until the lease was up the end of February. I stayed there until that time, then placed my belongings in storage. This amounted to eight boxes plus my winter clothes. I felt joyously unencumbered!

A short trip to Mexico early in March was followed by a longer one to the San Francisco Bay Area in California. I stayed away from metropolitan areas as much as possible, but to meet the Oughten House Publisher of *The Crystal Stair,* I had to journey into this densely populated area. Robert Gerard and I made a good connection by mail and phone and I volunteered to work with him for a couple of weeks. He and his wife offered me lodging and welcomed me like family.

The publishing operation, which was outgrowing their home, was a base for more than the printed word. The phone rang and rang with calls from people all over the world. People transformed by Oughten House books. People with ascension manuscripts to submit. People guided to send loving energy. This was not some small, obscure publishing venture. This was a starseed operation bursting with ever expanding consciousness, a swirling vortex of ascension movement energies.

There were the classical third dimensional difficulties challenging Rob, but he would stay with it until he dropped or ascended. I was exposed to numerous views on ascension through other writings and people. I let them filter through my consciousness, relating least to the notion of space ship *rescues.* Anything is possible. Earth is a free will zone where we can choose any reality we want. But, tired as I was, I did not perceive Earth as an awful place to be saved from and the more spiritually conscious I became, the more I cherished the planet.

A new book, *An Ascension Handbook,* had just arrived from the printers and I helped get it out to distributors and to customers. I started reading this work by Tony Stubbs a few nights after my arrival. Here were constructs I could relate to! My resonance and excitement grew as I read and journaled late into the night. Suddenly, I knew what ascension is about for me! Suddenly, I resolved the seeming contradiction of feeling called to leave Earth and feeling called to serve her. *She* is ascending! My service was to participate in this phenomenal process! We, Mother Earth and her children, Gaia and her Priest-esses, were rising out of an old field of density. We were ascending into lighter vibrational fields by activating our mental, emotional, and physical planes with spiritual consciousness!

I joyfully rocked back and forth on the bed, hugging my journal. *Dear, Sweet Journal. My treasured companion. I am so much more aware because of you. Thank you! Thank you!*

An Ascension Journal! Why not create a journal for others? I could share the journal writing techniques and my own ascension entries. This could assist users in channeling their spirit-self to receive guidance regarding their own personal and planetary ascension process. Format impressions pressed on my consciousness. I wrote until dawn. What was coming through would add the much needed dimension of the Sacred Feminine to the ascension movement and trigger awareness that Earth is a Living Goddess on her own ascension journey.

I awoke feeling alert after only two hours of sleep. It was St. Patrick's Day. The *wearing of the green* day. Images of Green Man danced in my head. I wanted to frolic in a grove. To dance and sing. It was great to be alive on Planet Earth!

Later that day, I made a stronger commitment to the ascension process by financially investing as a Literary Producer with Oughten House. I worked a few hours in the office, then went to the public library to continue working on my ascension journal. The first draft was joyfully completed in a few days. I took a couple more days to input it on an Oughten House computer and run a hard copy for Rob to review. It was time for me to leave, promising to come back in summer.

I wanted to be at VisionPoint for Easter Week. My yearning for Vision-Point intensified during this Holy Season when the potent Christian Mysteries were activated. Graham and I had consecrated the land as a Sacred Site on Easter Sunday, 1986. Good Friday was the day I died each year to that which no longer served. My focused intent was always greatest on this land.

VisionPoint never disappointed me! Death, resurrection, renewal, and rebirth awaited me there. Christianity was hanging on the cross and missed out on the Resurrection and the Ascension. I did not plan to miss out, and I stood on Initiation Knoll and proclaimed as much to the Four Directions. Then I rededicated the knoll as *Ascension Knoll*.

I still felt stymied by my sense that Graham and I had an unfulfilled destiny to complete, but had exhausted our capacities to pursue it. We could not transcend the limits of our third dimensional relationship. Efforts to do so continued to drain us. I often felt so *not me* around him. Who was this woman at such odds over land we both loved? Whomever she was, she was again returning to Tucson without resolving the matter of shared stewardship of VisionPoint.

I spent the rest of April and most of May in Tucson. This was a pit stop. Time to reorient. Would I spend the summer at VisionPoint or travel more? No inner direction surfaced so I stayed put in the homes of one sister or another. Though my outer involvements were minimal, I was working hard on the inner. My December astrological reading had also revealed that 1993 would be a time to face more of my shadow and finish with dysfunctional patterns. As advised, I was *fighting the good fight.*

Suddenly, the war was over. I woke up crying the morning of May 30. Guidance was to sign my VisionPoint interest over to Graham. A seven year cycle together had ended. The energy allotment for our process was expended. Our enmeshment must not continue into the next cycle. I needed to put all my energy and attention into healing and advancing. The Guidance was unquestionable. I set this action in motion the same day and felt great freedom. Momentarily, I flashed on the possibility that Graham would economically compensate me, providing the means to obtain land for the work with Gaia and Green Man. Just as quickly, I allowed that possibility to drop away. All our attempts to reach economic resolve had generated greater conflict. I needed to continue on course without expectations. What would be, would be.

Now my affairs were truly clear and current. I did have moments of mourning, but early in June I experienced a primal healing by participating in a Theater of the Earth workshop. This week long event was held at the beautiful Rim Institute in northern Arizona. Earth artist and performer Vijali Hamilton asked our group three questions: 1) What is our Source? 2) What is our sickness? and 3) What is our healing? At the end of the week, we were to perform our answers. The questions and answers activated an inner process for me that culminated in a performance that transformed me on a cellular level.

The workshop audience sat *in the world* on one side of a creek bed. On the other side, I, painted like an amoeba, curled up *in the void.* Pulsating. Pulsating. Slowly, I emerged into greater awareness. Lethargically, I stretched, found my voice, and spoke. "I come from nothing . . . from no-thing . . . from no-thing-ness."

Gradually, I evolved into greater awareness and moved to the other side, *into the world.* I took great delight in declaring, "I come from nothing, to something . . . to some-thing . . . some-one . . . some-thing-ness." I eagerly explored the state of *thing-ness* that I had entered.

But soon my wondrous awe of somethingness diminished and the sickness overtook me. I clutched at everyone and everything in sight. I shouted, "My sickness is holding on . . . attaching to something . . . to someone. Clutching! Holding ON!"

Exhausted, I cried out for healing and heard to *let go.* Then I knew, "My healing, our healing, is come-ing to some-one . . . some-thing . . . fluidly . . . freely . . . without attaching . . . without holding on."

I experienced somethingness anew and lovingly released it. I *allowed* life to flow through me. "Now I am free to re-turn to Source, to *nothing*, from which I came." I returned to the Beginning. There I stopped performing, resting in the Creative Void until it was real and timely for me to perform again.

Graham and I had clutched at each other and VisionPoint by holding onto expectations of how our marriage and stewardship *should* look. We had not known how to let Life flow freely through our relationship to each other or the land. Thus both relationships sickened. I had let go. Now I would rest in the Void.

In the early stages of our relationship, Graham had asked his Higher Self if it was right for us to commit to *being in relationship*. He mailed me a written copy of the response. The Higher Self perspective was that we would learn together and life for us would be good provided there were:

NO Rules
   Agreements
   Promises
   Expectations

My eyes immediately saw the word that the capital letters formed. The message from the higher dimension was NO RAPE! Graham had not noticed the word formation, but when I pointed it out we both saw the significance of the Guidelines presented to us. We committed to *being in relationship*, and immediately proceeded to set **R**ules, make and break **A**greements and **P**romises, and to have major **E**xpectations of the relationship and each other. **RAPE**. In the letting go, there were many lessons to integrate about our time together.

As I traveled in the months ahead, I knew I needed to let go of Vision-Point and open to more of Earth's wonder and beauty. I needed to fully embrace the sacredness of all that is the Earth. Arizona's Grand Canyon. Utah's fertile valleys. Colorado's spectacular Rockies. Wyoming's Grand Tetons. Oregon's wet, green lushness. California's amazing diversity. Visits to these magnificent places were enhanced by visits with old friends and meetings with new ones. Further, there was a workshop intensive with healer Hannah Kroger and a return trip to Oughten House. There I signed a publishing contract for *My Ascension Journal*. My travels always expanded my awareness of the multi-dimensional nature of life and I felt most grateful for every opportunity to honor my questing spirit.

I found my way back to my VisionPoint mountain in August, but not to the land herself. I camped in a densely treed area several miles from VisionPoint and came to know the mountain in new ways. I spent considerable time with friends, but withdrew into the Inner Realms as the August 15 observance day of Mary's ascension neared, followed the next day by my seven-year ordination anniversary as her Initiate. I spent this time in deep communion with this beloved Goddess who held the Immaculate Concept of humanity and Earth's ascension. Again she told me that she would like me to say *yes* to the Sacred Work. *Yes*, to staying with the Planet's process for another decade. Again, I responded, *Yes. Yes, of course.* I so loved the privilege of fully participating in the Creation Process that my spirit was, perhaps, all too quick to volunteer as it had done in the Beginning Times. Now my body was demanding more regard for its essential part in the plan. This decade would be different. I would be more attentive to the rest and play aspects of the Divine Design. And this Beloved Mother and Teacher informed me that I would receive advance training in the powers of focused concentration and experience greater blending between my internal and external realities, between the spiritual and material worlds. This alone would be restful!

Summer came and went. Autumn found me back in the Colorado Rockies. I had heard of a White Buffalo on a ranch near Crested Butte. Not one, but six, mixed in a herd of brown buffaloes! The papa, two mamas, and two of the calves had some buff coloring, but the smallest calf was very white. I was ecstatic! No humans were in sight to ask permission to enter the land, but I had not come this far to turn away. I got as close as I could without entering the barb wire range that contained them. The buffaloes were not free, but they were returning. My pilgrimage, begun in my White Buffalo van in early September of 1990, was now complete in late September of 1993. The Great Spirit had guided me to the White Buffalo Calf. I had been given a sign that I was *on the path of revelation and truth.* I gave great thanks!

I cried myself to sleep that night camped under tall golden aspens by a stream. This would be my last night sleeping in my van where I could gaze out of curtain free windows at the stars and moon and rising sun. The next few nights, I would be in Flagstaff in Maya's new home, then back to Tucson for the winter. I did not fare well out-of-doors in cold weather and knew I must again seek warmer shelter. But I dreaded becoming house and city bound again. Surely, there was a better way!

ॐ

The housing situation that opened its doors to me even before my return to Tucson certainly was not a statement of living differently, but indications were clear that this was where I was to winter. I was grateful to quickly resettle in the guest house belonging to a close friend. But in suburbia? I knew what my next lesson would be.

I had lived in Tucson in the early seventies and my life then was alive with cultural diversity. My workplace had a wonderful mixture of Mexicans, Chicanos, Native Americans, blacks, whites, and a Korean woman who was one of my best friends. We were all friends and often socialized together. My civil rights activism, that began in the sixties, was based on a love for multiplicity as much as on disdain for discrimination. My rather successful attempts to teach my Korean and Mexican friends English had motivated me to get a teaching credential when I moved to California. And the rich international flare of Los Angeles and of my classroom compensated for much of the urban madness.

When guidance came to return to Tucson in the nineties, I thought I would be coming home, but the world I had left behind no longer existed for me. The world that opened up to me was filled with white women. Interactions in this segregated environment stirred old memories. Much of my life, I have felt like a woman of color trapped in a confining white culture and a white body that constricted the flow of her sensual spirit. I tended to be much more attracted to men of color, connected in body, heart, and soul, than to white males living in their heads. For years, I appreciated hearing friends from other cultures say that I was "one of them." Then came a political rally when a Chicano brother, introducing me as a political rally speaker, said, "She's really a Chicana. She just looks white." Suddenly, I felt sick. What once was taken as a compliment, now made me ill. I did not have the courage then to say what I was feeling. I am white. If I am anti-white, I am anti-myself. If racial harmony is ever to exist on the planet, people of all races have to feel good about their heritage and the heritages of all people. That rally was the last time I was not a white woman. I made myself accountable for my whiteness, be it deemed good or bad.

An earlier realization had been that I did not like women; that I valued myself more because men told me I was different from other women. I later realized this was because I was more in touch with the male principle than the feminine. I was animus driven, yet *knew my place*. This changed when I began bonding with minority, lesbian, and low-income white women around political issues, for this led to bonding around our personal lives. For us, the personal *was* political. For us, mutual trust and support were survival issues. Another realization dawned. What was this deep internalized feeling that it was not okay to be who or what I am? This contempt of and separation from self? If I did not like women, I did not love myself. I began to love and respect these sisters, and thus myself.

Now my life no longer revolved around the political. It was centered in the spiritual. The women in my new world of Tucson were white and spiritual. They, too, heard the Call of the Goddess. These women were in my life to teach me how to love myself in deeper ways. But my economic views still created separation when I was in the homes of sisters who had mainstream lifestyles. I did not care less about them for living as they did. I just could not see meaning in their lives. Now, living in the suburban guest house of a close friend, I would have a chance to find out.

One of the things I love most about doing the Dance to Mend the Sacred Hoop is that it mends the Sacred Hoop torn by racial separation. To do the Dance is to cellularly reunite all peoples, bringing body, mind, spirit, and heart into that reunification. Turning to the each of the Four Directions, I honor the truth and gifts of the root race of that Direction. Thus the Truth and the Gifts of the Great Spirit can be remembered and received. The yellow race in the East, the people of the spirit. The black race of the South, the people of the body. The red race of the West, the people of the heart. The white race of the North, the people of mind. Each time I turned to the North, I had a deeper understanding of how much I yet had to mend within myself about my own race. Everyone, everything has a place in Creation. The foundational cornerstones of the white culture in these United States were mind, machines, materialism, and money. What are the Higher Truth and Greater Gifts contained in these cornerstones? As I found places for my few belongings in my furnished winter home, I knew I had an opportunity to heal my unresolved issues about my race, my culture, my country. I had an opportunity to mend the sacred hoop of my own soul.

Once unpacked, I opened to Guidance regarding my next step —which needed to generate income. I definitely needed to face my money issues head on as I reentered life in Tucson. Throughout my travels, I stayed open to the possibility of relocating. People were awakening everywhere and I stayed attentive for indications that I was to start over elsewhere, but none appeared. However, I was glad to be back. This desert oasis always welcomed me home and allowed me to express at more evolved levels of being. This time, Tucson was vibrating at a higher frequency. Three new metaphysical bookstores and a metaphysical paper sprang up over the summer to prove it. Each enterprise showed signs that they would prosper.

Books with new, transformational vibrations continued to impact and guide my way. The message of *The Celestine Prophecy* by James Redfield and the process of *Stepping Free of Limiting Patterns with Essence Repatterning* by Pat McCallum became the next texts in my personal curriculum. They also turned out to be avenues for income.

By the time I finished reading the Third Insight of the nine given in the Prophecy, I knew where the book was leading. I jumped ahead to the final chapter and, sure enough, the Ninth Insight had to do with ascension! *Ascension* was not the word utilized, but there was no mistaking the book's message of humanity's progression into realms of higher consciousness.

Many of my friends were impacted by the Insights and I offered to facilitate an interactive study group. Fourteen of us met for ten expansive weeks. I received requests to do another study group, then another. My favorite insights were the nature related ones. Meeting indoors was limiting and I felt inspired to offer an all day retreat. This *Day of Insights* attracted over forty people who eagerly packed into our meeting space. Soon we spread out in the surrounding desert area for personal experiences with nature. Everyone came back together energized, just as the book indicated they would. I was so grateful to help others reawaken to nature's aliveness. And I was having great fun in the process! Later, I coordinated a weekend nature retreat called *Life Is A Mystical Experience*. My awareness that this is so was increasing daily.

The repatterning process was hard, very personal, work. But it, too, was fun and was something I had requested. I had facilitated journal writing processes for seven years. Another cycle had ended. It had been essential for women to reclaim our voices by telling our stories. Journal writing was an empowering way to break the silence of our lives and to process our experiences. But by the time I left Earth Song, I knew all the stories. The underlying themes and patterns were all the same. Only the names, times, and places differed. We needed new stories! New patterns!

I informed the Universe that I wanted to be shown new ways to work with the written word. *My Ascension Journal* was one way. Essence Repatterning was the next. It amplified the mind research and work I had done as an educator in the early 1980s. I had been convinced that teaching the fundamentals of how the mind works would transform education. I was delighted to again delve into the realms of the subconscious, conscious and superconscious mind.

Being highly self-directed, I worked intently with this process of re-framing limiting, outmoded patterns to create new internal circuitry of evolved patterns. My perceptions began to shift dramatically. Sometimes, this led to dramatic improvement in my relationships and behaviors. Other times, it was clear I had to walk away from certain relationships. I peeled away layers of old beliefs in lack and limitation, fears that life is not safe and feelings of unworthiness. I cleared the tracks of my woundedness and laid new tracks for healing and creative expansion. The harder I worked, the easier the process became. I felt frequent cellular shifts and an increasing sense of buoyancy.

When sharing my excitement about the process with friends, many asked me to assist them in their own repatterning work. Word spread, and once again, I was doing work I loved at deep interpersonal levels. Learning and teaching. Teaching and learning.

But something else was in the air. I sensed that there was something more to do with many old friends and numerous new ones met through the Insights and Essence Repatterning. Others sensed it, too. Some were getting inner guidance to *See Nicole . . . Work with Nicole*. We repatterned and worked with the Insights, waiting for *something more* to reveal itself.

In the meantime, I continued clearing out my old mental house. I was intent on working with the astrological influences for 1993 that heralded an end to old dysfunctional patterns. Unresolved family of origin issues had dramatically resurfaced during the year and called for final clearing. I had turned away from *The Father* to be about my *Mother's business* and torn the fabric of relationship with my Heavenly and Earthly families. More mending to do. I spent New Year's Eve with the book *God I Am* by Peter Erbe. As I read, I repatterned my false perceptions that were brought to light in this material guided by Isis, Immanuel, St. Germain, and Archangel Michael. I resonated most profoundly with the perspective that everything is energy and all energy needs validation simply because it exists. By invalidating anything or anyone, I created the sense of separation and denied the holiness of All That Is. On New Year's Day, I awakened with truer perceptions and spent the morning ritualistically acknowledging my own Divinity and that of my family and all the people in my life, past, present, and future. I affirmed our right to be different *and* our Oneness in the Dance of Creation. Yes, 1994 was sure to be a new dawning.

ⓐ

Glena took strongly to Essence Repatterning and I became increasingly involved with her process regarding the business. This gave me many opportunities to review my lessons as she went through her version of them. Earth Song was now Inner Dimensions. This name, the merchandise, and programming now reflected her spiritual focus. Early in the new year, she started talking about being ordained to formalize her ministry. It took us a while to perceive the obvious. Of course! I could ordain her in the Fellowship of Isis.

As we explored what that process would look like, we talked of forming a circle of Priestess Initiates. Separately, we made a list of potential participants and came up with the same names. I realized that the women who would come together in this circle had been the other Priestesses with me in the tunnel! Truly, this was the time of the Return of the Goddess!

Glena contacted the women on the list to invite them to a meeting to discuss formation of a Priestess circle. We agreed not to promote participation, relying instead on each woman's inner response. We were to meet at Inner Dimensions on March 7, 1994, two years after I had rented the space as Earth Song. Perhaps, Earth Song seeds would grow!

I asked for a sign to assure me that it was appropriate for me to facilitate this group process of awakening the Priestess. The meeting date arrived and no sign had manifested. That afternoon I distributed flyers for my next *Celestine Prophecy* activity. My last stop was at Awakenings Book Store. I felt inclined to browse and quickly spotted the book *Isis and Osiris* by Jonathan Cott. It had just arrived the day before. I opened directly to the chapter entitled "The Fellowship Of Isis At Clonegal Castle"! A picture of Lady Olivia and Lord Lawrence were on the next page, followed by a lengthy interview with Lady Olivia. I did not need more of a sign than this!

I was amazed, but not surprised, as the temple room at Inner Dimensions filled up that night. The women listened receptively as Glena and I described the process leading up to the meeting. I read the tunnel memory and it became more alive for me. Each woman then spoke of why she had come. Some remembered the tunnel. Others had no recall of it, but remembered other Priestess lifetimes. Still others had no memories, but felt this meeting would transform their lives. The energy built with each woman's sharing. I felt an exhilaration I had not known in this lifetime. This was the *something more.*

As each woman shared her truth, she triggered greater awareness of our collective truth as women. Many of the women had been part of a Sex and Spirituality discussion group that I had recently facilitated at Inner Dimensions. Glena and I had both been impacted by Clysta Kinstler's book *The*

Moon Under Her Feet. It is a compelling telling of the life of Mary Magdalene as High Priestess and Divine Consort to Yeshua the Christ. Our intention statement was: "We choose to know ourselves as divine aspects of the God/Goddess, fully attuned to the sacredness of our spiritual/sexual/sensual natures."

In speaking together of the role of a Priestess, we talked of her function as the High Priestess of Love, the Magdalene Protectress of the Sexual Fires. She who wed Yeshua, the anointed King, the Holy Bridegroom, who died that the people might live. There are those who would still stone the Sacred Prostitute and Temple Dancers have been relegated to lowly positions as strip tease dancers. We all felt the permeation of the Madonna/Whore complex in every cell of our bodies. Female sexuality had been maligned, abused, objectified. Our very bodily functions were cheapened. The miracle of the blood mysteries was cursed.

The ways of midwives and witches had returned. Women Priests were ordained in the Episcopal Church. Was the slow re-emergence of the Priestess due to the pervasive cultural repression of the Sacred Erotic? In the times of the Goddess Past, Priestesses filled many functions not directly linked to sexuality, but every Priestess knew the electric serpent, the kundalini fire that connects one with the creative source of the universe. Full re-emergence of the Goddess Present implies a re-awakening to these mysteries in ways appropriate to these times and our lives. A common thread running through our discussion was that we wanted to reclaim the sacredness of our bodies, the sacredness of woman's place in the worldly scheme of things.

We had many more questions than answers. Clearly, we were engaging in a discovery process activated by our collective inquiries and experiences. Glena and I had not worked out details prior to the meeting. We knew to wait until there was evidence of interest. I had, however, written out a nine-month Awakening The Priestess Process to have something tangible to propose. Several women wanted to commit that night, but I asked that everyone sleep on the proposal at least three nights. I knew activation of this process would change our lives more than any of us realized and the decision to commit could not be casually made.

I was too energized to sleep when I got home. Guidance was to read my dissertation over in its entirety. I had not read it through for over a year and hoped reading it would make me sleepy. Quite to the contrary! So much that had faded from consciousness during the past two years now had new life. Without referring to the curriculum described therein, I had recreated it in the Awakening the Priestess proposal. The past year was the gestation period I had been told needed to occur! I had not dropped the proverbial ball. Inadvertently, I had *allowed* needed time for the next development phase to emerge.

I rejoiced in the perfection of The Process. I imprinted the matrix in the third dimension by writing the dissertation. Then Earth Song and I planted the seeds. Glena relieved me so I could rest and be renewed before undertaking my next step. She took the crucial role of physically holding Sacred Space wherein our Priestess Selves could safely emerge from the tunnel. Since my return, we had artfully played off each other's consciousness until we uncovered the pathway. With due regard for our persistence, it was clear that there was a Guiding Force greater than the power or our personal selves.

A second meeting was held March 17, 1994 for women who could not make the meeting on the 7th. By the following week, a dozen women had informed me that they wanted to be in the Priestess Circle. I had facilitated many groups for many people, but this was different. I did not know exactly how, but this was very different!

I needed to be in nature to prepare. Only there could I truly clear, energize, and renew myself. I packed up the White Buffalo for a week and headed for the St. David area in southeastern Arizona. The first day, I had ongoing discussions in my head with people in Tucson. Greatly annoyed, I shouted, "Shut up! I want to be here now!" The chatter stopped immediately! The Inner Stillness I needed to hold the focus for this Sacred Work was firmly established.

I was given two major inner work assignments to undertake later in the week in the Chiricahuas. This Geronimo stronghold called to me even louder than Greece had. Every aspect of my being felt clearer as I drove closer to this National Park. When I parked in my campsite and stepped out of the van, I instantly trembled and cried. My feet came alive. I knew this land and it knew me.

As I write, I feel the same high degree of alertness I felt then. When I lived there, not so long ago, as an Apache, I needed keenness of mind, body, and spirit to survive. Now hiking the trails through this Wonderland of Rocks, I welcomed the renewed sharpening of my senses. This made the inner work easy. My first assignment was to list everyone who had ever hurt me, what they had done to me, and the good qualities I saw in them. This done, I blessed and released them. Next, I reversed the process, listing everyone I had ever hurt and what I had done to them. I wrote down my good qualities, then blessed and forgave myself. As was the case in all deep healing work I have done, I found that the greatest woundings were those that repressed the flow of love and creative expression. I would never truly heal until these channels were fully opened.

I ritualistically burned the lists in my campfire, asking the alchemy of the fire to transmute the negative energies and redirect them for the Greatest Good. Guidance indicated that this would minimize the amount of projection I might do on the Priestess Process or on the participants.

My second task was to focus on each Sacred Sister who had participated in either of the Priestess meetings and release her from all soul contracts we had made in any lifetime. This was to insure that whatever transpired between us in the here and now was free of emotionally enmeshed commitments tied to the past. There was no more time left to engage in activities that did not support our present Truth. I slept soundly my last night in this homeland. I awakened with the clarity of consciousness needed to be a clear channel for The Process.

Soon after my return to Tucson, two of the women informed me that they would not be participating. They felt awkward about having felt so sure, then changing their minds, and were glad to hear of my releasing process. Now we were each free to continue unencumbered by ancient contracts that were no longer viable.

ം

The eleven of us who felt guided to proceed met on April 7. We were giddy with anticipation and apprehension. We joked about being closeted Priestesses and whether or not to use the "P" word. One of the women was openly *coming out*. Another had decided not to tell her husband yet. She did not want to risk diminishing her process by his potential disapproval. Several of the women expressed deep fears tied into past life memories of being burned at the stake, having their hands cut off for healing others, being ostracized by their community. Another expressed her awareness that she had abused her powers in the past. Though we did not want to cloak ourselves in secrecy, we agreed it was essential to honor the privacy of each participant.

We did not know where this would lead, and we were relatively comfortable allowing the process to unfold. However, each of us knew this was a step we needed to take wherever it might lead. Strangest of all, without any of us truly knowing what it means to be a Priestess now, many women feared they were unworthy of whatever it was.

Whenever our talk became too amorphous, I brought up aspects of the nine-month format. The design was to focus for a trimester on *knowing ourselves*. The second trimester on *knowing ourselves through nature*. The final three months on *co-creating ritual* relevant to our lives and these times. Through this Process, the Priestess within each of us would reveal herself and her contemporary function.

From my perspective, Priestessing, past or present, honors all Life as sacred. The Priestess interfaces with life at the non-judgmental level of patterns, energy flows, and vibrational fields rather than the judgmental level of personalities and issues. For this reason, I suggested that everyone work with the constructs of Essence Repatterning and the energy related insights of *The Celestine Prophecy*.

I put great stock in *intentionality* and urged everyone to hold clear intent to align with Priestess consciousness. I shared that when perplexed about a course of action in difficult situations, I often inwardly asked myself, "What would a Priestess do?" This question and the ensuing answers always pulled me back into alignment with the clarifying Priestess vibration. Many women posed the question for themselves right then. They automatically shifted into graceful postures and a light appeared in their eyes. We were engaging a very potent energy field to assist our souls on their journeys back to Wholeness. I fully intended to play for real. And so did they.

Their Initiation would take place on Beltane Eve, April 30, 1994. This ceremony and the energies of this time of ancient fire and fertility festivals would fully activate the Awakening the Priestess vibrational field for each woman. What the awakening experience looked like would vary with each one. Ordination, for those who stayed with the process, was set for Candlemas, February 2, 1995. This ceremony will activate the Priestess archetype. The Priestess would bring the woman into alignment with her Goddess Self and her world would never be the same.

Particulars of what has transpired since that magical Beltane Eve is beyond the scope of this writing. There are stories within this story, scriptures within this scripture. They will be written and spoken of by those living them. In time, I will write more. For now, I can only offer a general overview of the Awakening the Priestess Process and delve into my own process around it. I have been guided to a higher level of facilitator consciousness. I am fortifying my capacity to hold and harmonize group energy and to finely attune with subtle energies. This work affords me the opportunity to develop my powers of focused concentration by holding the vision of each woman's awakening. Most importantly, I am learning how to allow infinite space for each woman to awaken in her own time and her own way. This is simply a matter of tuning in as the Goddess guides The Process.

Each woman sets the tone for her private session. Often this means listening to her talk for hours at a time with very little input on my part. I simply hold sacred space for her to give voice to her own process, trusting she will hear her own answers. She does – in her own time and way. Just given the opportunity to speak of what is going on in her life, in her being, without being challenged, invalidated, or directed, she experiences her own knowing and becomes her own witness. Giving Voice to her Inner Knowing, often unspoken in this lifetime, she becomes more conscious and reclaims her True Self. By simply being PRESENT for each woman, each circle, and The Process, we awaken. By being clear in intention and attentive to what transpires, we remember. By BE-ing, we transcend.

With the wisdom of Sophia, I do not tell anyone how I think they need to be as a Priestess. This is something only they know. I do share what being a Priestess means to me and strive to create settings and experiences that will activate the subtle Priestess vibrational field. The only *advice* I give is *go within*. The Essence Self resides in the Stillness as the Keeper of each one's Truth. On the basis of profoundly affirming experience, I assure them of the sanctity of the Silence, of Sacred Inner Space, where the inspiring guidance of the Priestess Self abides. In private sessions, I sometimes ask if they would like to hear what I have done in situations similar to theirs and/or what I am picking up on as I listen. I seldom give voice to my images or impressions unless they ask for them or without first asking if they want me to share them. The Goddess Within each woman is in charge. I ask for an opening, a sign, if it is for the Greatest Good for me to make strong suggestions. I am clear that my function is to consistently hold the vision of the Priestess awakening in the consciousness of each woman no matter what is outpicturing to the contrary.

By stepping back to create more space for each woman to have direct experience in tapping into her own inner resources, I witness transformations beyond the scope of my imaginings. In supporting others to be True to Self, I support myself in my living, being, my Truth. By doing unto others as I would have them do unto me, a world in which I can thrive is emerging. Together, we co-create an environment of shared Truths that catapult us into a more magnificent Whole rather than reducing ourselves to our lowest common denominator. In this Sacred Space, we establish personal conviction that we will never again diminish our Creative Selves by being molded into someone else's truth. In this Creative Process, I become the loom, the weaver, and the woven. I do not copy the work of another. I stay attentive to what is trying to express through me, through us, and wait for the inner impulse indicating how, where, and when it is to be woven into the tapestry.

In group sessions, to sustain the integrity of The Process, I am often more directive, but I try not to impose my perspective. When called to do so, I speak, then allow space for responses. Always, I strive to be true to my own process by not engaging in activities that to do not support my growth and resonance with the Sacred in me, in all. By being real, being genuine, I vibrate in ways that draw forth the True Self in others that we might become a resonating core. Primarily, I work with the energy flows. Given my highly catalytic and reflective energies, I naturally facilitate, orchestrate, and harmonize energies. I have learned to shut down this capacity when energies are too discordant or fragmented for me to handle. However, the Priestess Process is graduate degree work for me. Through it, I am earning my *Crystal Priestess* title. Many nights after group sessions, I am awake for hours learning how to harmonize the group energies with the Essence of the Priestess Oversoul. Sometimes this means I drive for a while before going home. Other times, I go straight home and dance or simply sit with the feelings, often experiencing hot body temperatures as I burn off dross and transmute shadow energies. I am always aided by the Invisible Ones who facilitate my process. Sometimes, I collapse in bed exhausted, adamantly declaring "I don't want any part of this Priestessing stuff anymore!" Often, I reach a natural high and joyfully jump in bed smiling, even laughing – feeling the exhilaration of our ascension in consciousness.

Frequently, my Sacred Sisters voice appreciation for my lack of ego involvement in the process. I rarely feel any. It is a very peaceful feeling to simply allow The Process to unfold. It is easier to take responsibility for my own reactiveness than to arrogantly assume I know how others should live their lives. This has not always been the case in my life, but I am grateful it is so now. Given relationship enmeshments with my sons or mates, it has been hard to separate what was my life, theirs, ours. Not yet having a strongly developed sense of self, I could not tell who was trying to live whose life. This was where ego became involved.

In my van travels, the possessions I took along became metaphors for my emotional and psychological *stuff*. What I took with me was a smaller version of my stuff. What I took into homes of friends when I slept in a spare bed, was yet a smaller version. One night when I lay down to sleep in a particularly cluttered room, I noted I was not bothered by my friend's stuff. Everything I owned fit in my van. Everything I needed for the night, fit in a small pack. What she owned overflowed a house. And it was just fine! Somehow, I made a clear metaphorical transference regarding my stuff and the stuff of others. Metaphorical or literal, it was just fine! As long as I did not mix metaphors, I could handle my own baggage and be fine with whatever metaphors others wanted to use as analogies for their personal process. This liberating awareness helps me stay clear in relating to my sisters.

I am extraordinarily grateful to be an intimate part of each woman's process. It is a great privilege to be in intimate proximity to a sister's process. To learn her lessons, feel her feelings, think her thoughts, as if my own. For she is a face of the Goddess of 10,000 faces and we are reflections of each other. As each one claims her beauty and her truth, I become more beautiful and able to live my truth. As each one actualizes her gifts and talents, I express my gifts and talents at higher levels. As each one softens into the depths of the feminine mysteries, I am more immersed in them. As each one becomes more grounded in her convictions, I become more rooted in mine. I cherish our bond as sisters. I cherish my bond to the Goddess through them.

One of the most challenging and rewarding aspects of The Process has been for each of us to learn to truly receive. Giving is easy, too easy for us. Receiving is another matter. Truly receiving even a simple "thank you," without deflecting it has required major repatterning. The Goddess does not deprive her children or her Priest-esses. If we continue to block the abundance of the Universe, of our own Earth Mother, how can we ever become fully actualized Beings? As our appreciation for one another grows, we note how badly we feel if someone unconsciously rejects our expressed appreciation. Through this mirroring, we are learning how to joyfully give and joyfully receive.

During the first trimester, each woman has a turn to tell the story of her sacred journey. She is honored in a foot washing ritual and given a small gift from her sisters. The stories are cathartic for the teller and the listeners. They bring each woman to her place of *now*. They are healing. Empowering. Unifying. Moving. But what touches me most is watching each woman receive. Awkwardly, at first. Gradually . . . timidly . . . opening to receive the appreciation and attention given to them. Finally, absorbing the nurture of being honored for herself.

If working with this group of Priestesses was all there was to The Process, I would be quite content. But this is just the beginning. Other women approached me to start another circle and thirteen new women were Initiated at the Autumn Equinox. A third circle of twelve was activated in Northern Arizona on December 12 and a fourth circle is preparing for its Initiation at the March New Moon 1995. Most of the women in the first circle see their ordination as their real beginning, not the end. Interest is even being expressed by women outside the state and the country. All of this has evolved by word-of-mouth. No advertising or marketing approaches are being implemented. The women are simply responding to the inner Call of the Goddess.

A Sisterhood of women ages twenty-eight to sixty-five in all shapes and sizes has formed. We have become increasingly comfortable about acknowledging ourselves as Priestesses — for this is what we are. The matrix of the Sisterhood will symbolically take form with the ordination of the fourth circle. Then the four foundational cornerstones will be in place for the Shrine of the Sacred Feminine represented by the Ceremonial Tent co-created by Priestess Initiate Leah and the Goddess Sarasvati. At this point, I believe The Process will evolve into other forms of expression.

The biggest hump that each circle and each woman encounters is taking individual initiative for amplifying The Process. I have no intention of becoming a project director or Mother Superior or of trying to meet everyone's personal needs in the limited time periods we are together as a group. I activate, facilitate, witness, and support. I hold the loom and weave the threads of our journey into the tapestry of our Divine Design. I celebrate each woman's emergence and give thanks when she reveals the mysteries encoded in the scrolls of her consciousness. As this happens, The Process takes on a life of its own. The Sisterhood blossoms as each Priestess petal opens to the light. By training, assisting, and inspiring one another in the healing and creative arts, we co-create healing, creative lives for ourselves. Reiki initiations re-establish our direct hookups to Source. Bio-Magnetics, massage, Tantra, and Sacred Dance re-connect our bodies and spirits. We are becoming sisters/daughters/mothers/midwives/healers/Priestesses/goddesses to one another. We are fulfilling the primary purpose of every human — to find and express our True Selves. And it is good. Very good.

Not long ago, I wondered what this *Priestess stuff* was all about. Now my life is filled with Priestesses embodying the re-emerging Goddess. By coming together, we remember and activate the Divine Design. By joining hands and hearts, we heal our wounds and become our visions. By asking what it means to be a Priestess in these times, we co-create a New Earth Fulfilled. By honoring ourselves and each other, we honor the Goddess and make Her Presence known again. By living our individual truths, we reveal the many faces and aspects of the Goddess. By co-creating ceremonies that evolve out of our own experience and desire to celebrate Life, and that incorporate symbols relevant to our daily lives, we reclaim the sacredness of our bodies and our lives. We give form to that which we hold in consciousness and experience cellular transformation, deeper meaning to our lives, and a reconnection with Nature. By acknowledging one another as Priestesses, we create mirrors for our Priestess self and begin to see the Priestess in every woman and the Priest in every man. By finding our center as women, we can begin to reach out to the men in healthy, life affirming ways.

Our growing openness and honesty with one another reveals how sexually wounded we are. Rape. Incest. Sex without intimacy. Insensitive, de-womanized birthing and medical treatment. Being shamed for being sensual, sexual. Shamed for being cold, frigid. For bleeding. For feeling. For being affectionate with one another. Completely ostracized if sexual preference for women is one's truth. Because of the wounds, or perhaps startlingly in spite of them, there is a deep yearning to heal the separation between women and men by reclaiming the sacredness of our bodies and our sexuality . . . a deep yearning to express our fullness and our truth in our relationships with men.

Flo Calhoun's book, *I Remember Union*, speaks deeply to many of us. This story of Mary Magdalena affirms what we know — that we are part of the vision of peace and union between women and men, humanity and divinity. The 2000 year prophecy is being fulfilled within each of us and we will yearn no more.

We are also facing and healing the distrust women have in women. If I can not trust my own gender, how can I trust myself as a woman? If I do not love my sisters, how can I love myself? We are all struggling with issues of self-worth and self-love. And often we stumble over and on each other in our efforts to come together in unity and diversity. We all encounter difficulties in disengaging the old paradigm constructs of distrust, misconceptions, divisiveness, projections and fear. It is not always easy to have ultimate trust in The Process, knowing that everyone is doing the best she can to keep body and soul together while evolving. I give thanks that by bonding with my Sacred Sisters, I am feeling more trusting and worthy of love from myself and others.

The most profound expression of our bonding process, for me, is when we hold space for the spectrum of our differences. Invariably, when differences in approaches, appearances, lifestyles, wants, needs or beliefs arise, the women at either end of the spectrum fear rejection if they speak or act on their truth. Getting to the place where each of us feels appreciated and validated for who and how we are is intensely healing for all involved. A thread running through all our lives was the sense of being a misfit, of not belonging, of being *too* different. We have all known quiet desperation, depression, despair. We are all damaged by not being ourselves and by feeling we are damaging others when we are ourselves. Together, we were turning our lives around in celebration of our uniqueness and that of others.

Often, I detect our fear of our own power and note the ways we hold it back. Is it safe to express it? Will the price be too high? Will we be ridiculed or outcast? Will we abuse or misuse the power? Can we let go of our pictures of how we think things should be and feel? Matriarchs can be *power over* dominators, too. But I know we will move through those fears. We have a deep soul commitment to co-create safe space for our collective re-emergence. We do not have to step forth alone. We have all made the heroine's journey. Now we are fitting together the pieces of our individual journey to solve the mysteries of our lives. We are ready for a quantum leap. As each woman reclaims her authenticity and takes her sovereign place in the circle in *power with* consciousness, the synergy of our collective whole will be explosive. And we need an explosion to thrust ourselves into co-creative, life affirming realities. Then the question becomes, *Are we ready to experience our Magnificence? To fully experience the Magnificence of the Human Experience?*

The power of the circle is much more dynamic than the power of the follow-the-leader line. The circle forms a container or cauldron for the energies brought to it. And when those forming the circle harmonize the energies, what is co-created or brewed is infinitely more potent, more impacting, than what is produced by a hierarchy. That is why patriarchy is experiencing its demise. For Creation to continue we must reclaim the consciousness of cells or clusters of resonating energy.

Even while shedding the last vestiges of the old system, it has been hard to stop defining ourselves and our Sacred Work by what we *do* and to appreciate ourselves for who we *are*. Awakening the Priestess is not an *undertaking* or a project. It is an *inner sojourn*, a process of coming together to co-create and energize Sacred Space that is held in consciousness and sustains us when we are apart. It is about living life consciously and being in the NOW.

The more I expand in consciousness, the more I realize the puny-ness of my perspective of what is possible. As I work to remove limits from my consciousness, I see that even my most grandiose views of what might be are restricted by the limits of finite mind. I gladly and gratefully hold sacred space for our emergence that we might erupt into greater dimensions of being.

To fulfill my function in this Process, I consistently seek Inner Counsel. I trust the intricate perfection of The Process and surrender to it. I need to stay clear. I need greater self-knowing. I need to bear witness to The Process without projecting on others or losing my center while my sisters move through their awakening process. I need to know when to yield without losing my own integrity or the integrity of The Process. I need time to rest and play and forget all about this Priestess business. It is only one of endless ways to experience and express Creation. I tend to work twenty-five days a month, preparing for and facilitating group and private Priestess sessions, integrating the energies, writing an internal newsletter, rewriting this material, answering related letters and phone calls. It is my nature to be accessible. It is becoming my nature to balance my availability to others with time for myself. When I need privacy, I turn off the ringer on my phone and hang a colorful *Please Do Not Disturb* needlepoint sign on my door. This was lovingly and beautifully made for me by one of my Sacred Sisters. I reserve several days a month just for me when I do little inner or outer work. A monthly time off period is natural to woman's cycle to clear and review. I believe a reclaiming of the blood mysteries and woman's lodge consciousness will greatly benefit humankind.

Essence repatterning remains a primary tool for my inner work, greatly facilitating my capacity to be starkly honest with myself. New *text books* and opportunities have appeared as additional aids. My core issues were around my relationships to my body, my sons, money, and housing. Gentle, loving assistance came from the Pleiadian P'Taah who came into my life through the book *An Act of Faith* channeled by Jani King.

He is big on *feeling your feelings* and self-love. His gentle words guided me into a more committed and tender realm of connectedness with my soul and my body. I had already developed a meditation practice of sitting with my feelings. This evolved out of my need to work with my anger. My tendency had been to stuff it or dump it. Either way was a *no win* situation. I began simply sitting with my anger. Feeling it. Letting the adrenaline rush clear my consciousness. When someone triggered my anger, my initial reaction would be to feel angry at them. Sitting with this anger led me to anger toward myself for getting into the situation. Lingering below this anger were other feelings. Old feelings. Old pains. Old grief. I would feel them all.

Buried beneath all these feelings was an injured little girl who just wanted to love and be loved. She grew up to be a woman who wanted the same. I felt harmed more by not having open channels through which love could flow, than by any other tragedy in my life. My channels were blocked and corroded by past neglect, negation, invalidation, abuse, stress, unconsciousness, hate, fear, resentment, bitterness, pain, grief, loss, loneliness. The list was long. The blocks were many. I constructed some of the blocks. Some were constructed by others. I always had room for more wounds, but not for the goodness in my life. This I deflected due to a distorted sense of unworthiness.

Gradually, those channels are being reconstructed through my determined efforts to clear the past and to learn to love and accept myself. When I am living in the present, feeling my feelings, and loving myself, love freely flows through channels that were nearly shut down. Though I have been emotionally and physically separate from my parents, brothers, and former mates for years, I now think of them and feel profound universal love. I do not know if I will ever express this love to any of them directly. I am happy to simply be loving them in my heart. There, I even feel their love for me.

Feeling my body's feelings and tapping into its intelligence has been my most profound breakthrough in consciousness. P'Taah is a loving ally of the body. I am learning to be. It is astounding to realize how I have enslaved my body by my ideas, and dominated it with my mind. *Do this. Do that. Go here. Go there. No time to exercise, play, nap.* I have treated it like a robot instead of as the miracle it is. I have criticized and demeaned the way it looks and performs. I keep trying to *fix it — fix my hair, my face* – to conform to a cultural image I scorn. I try to *fix* the way my body functions and interfere with its natural capacity to regenerate itself and align with my mental, emotional, and spiritual bodies.

My loyal body is my life long friend and I have taken it for granted. It has been subject to my compulsions and addictions and is cautious about trusting me. Yet it is responsive to whatever attention, validation, and consideration I give. When I relate to my body's intelligence, it communicates very specifically. Body made it clear it does not want any more invasive healing techniques employed. No more needles poked into it by doctors, nurses, or acupuncturists. It responds well and happily to Bio-Magnetics, Reiki, massage, and no-force chiropractic treatments. It responds to kindness and looks and feels better than it has in years. I have developed a delicately balanced eco-system for my mental, emotional, spiritual, and physical bodies that I am steadily fortifying. I still have the lump in my breast and bless it for reminding me to nurture myself and be loving to my body. It will dissolve when I do not need to be reminded.

In many ways, I feel I have been as unconscious about how to relate to my children as I have been about my body. As an Initiate of Mary, I am being trained to hold the Immaculate Concept of the divine perfection of my sons' lives just as she was trained to hold it for her son. As an ordinary woman, I fear I am too weak to develop the Divine Mother's capacity not to give up regardless of what outpictured in her Beloved Son's life. Appearances indicate my sons' lives are lamentable. Old patterns were for me to intervene on their behalf. This translates to interfering and not letting them take full responsibility for their own lives, their own destinies.

But it is simplistic to only view our relationships through the lens of codependency. No other relationships in our lives have been of such duration. No other relationships taught or filled me as much. I served them by taking delight in watching them grow without turning my eyes away when I did not like what I saw. They served me by giving me reason to live when I had no other. They needed evidence that this burden was lifted from them. There had been so many voices of outer authority dictating how I should relate to my children. Dr. Spock, our family doctor, the parish Priest, conspired to drown out the quiet voice of mothering intuition and interfered with my capacity to parent at a soul level. If I turned away from our soul lessons together, they would crop up another time, another place.

Here were more lessons I had to get at a cellular level before their lives or mine could shift. Repatterning helped. Refining my capacity to hold space for the Priestesses to evolve in their own time and way helped. And my new friend P'Taah helped me to move through my fears, regrets, and not-good-enough mother guilt.

He is a wonderful promoter of the feminine energies of allowing, accepting, being. He points out that men and women have been working predominantly with the masculine energies of *controlling, judging and doing* for some two thousand years, and it is time for a change. His integrated androgynous energies helped me find peace as a mom, a Priestess, and an

Initiate of Mary. When I stopped *judging* Joel or Todd's lives as not working, I *accepted* life on life's terms, and stopped trying to *control* the situation or *do* something, anything, to make things better by my standards. I focused on *allowing* their lives to travel their own course. *Allow . . . ALLOW.* I love the vibrational feel of this word. It is so nurturing, so feminine. Simply saying the word triggers a positive cellular response.

My sons taught me a lot about allowing. Not so long ago, I chastised Joel for choices he was making. His quiet response was, "I'm being the best me I know how to be." Whoa! Each of us is *being the best me* we know how to be.

While worrying about what to *do* about a difficult situation Todd was facing, Guidance whispered, *If you stop trying to fix him, he can stop acting broken.* Allow . . . ALLOW.

It was hard to accept that I had not advanced further in separating my identity from my sons' despite the lack of Rites of Passages to assist mothers and sons in disengaging from their long term bonds. I saw their struggles as a reflection on me. *If I had been a more conscious mom, everything would be different.* In rewriting this work, I felt embarrassed when I got to the part dealing with the Death and Rebirth ritual just prior to my own ordination. That was three years earlier! I supposedly died to the old pattern of daughter/wife/mother to be reborn to the new pattern of Priestess. What a slow death!

I was not holding compassionate space for myself in which I could awaken in my own time and my own way. One ritual was not going to change my identity as a mother. An identity developed over decades that molded me into the Priestess I have become! It was time to revisit the tree that witnessed and supported my intent. I lived two blocks away from where I had performed the ritual and I went there immediately. As I again leaned against the tree, I reaffirmed my intention and got the lesson of being gentle with myself. I was an okay Priestess mom. The Priestess mom knows the divinity of her children and looks for a Higher Purpose in their challenges. The Priestess just needs to impersonally keep reminding the mom that there is a Greater Force guiding the process of her sons' lives. The mom needs to make the Priestess aware that this mothering business is hard work with very personal demands and rewards.

There was more to the lesson. It had to do with basic economics. Two years earlier, I realized the confusion I created for Joel and Todd as a single parent. When they were in crisis, Mom welcomed them back to the nest and nurtured them till they felt safe again. When it became clear they were getting too comfortable, she played Dad and booted them out on their own to become men. I shared this revelation in a private session with Brooke Medicine Eagle who guided me through a shamanic journey to integrate my mother/father aspects. The journey was an immediate success. I was able to lovingly work out an economic plan with my sons that would subsidize their income for a year while they were finding their way in the World.

The year was up. I was finally ready to surrender my parental responsibility to their true Source. This was a major letting go. Correspondingly, I experienced tremendous release. I now measure how well their lives are working based on my level of acceptance of their processes and, according to that criteria, they are doing quite well. And as is always the case, once I achieve inner resolve, outer conditions improve.

The financial assistance I offered my sons rose out of a strange mixture of love, guilt and fear. I love my sons dearly and love contributing to their lives. But fear was the real issue. At a spiritual and intellectual level, I believe in a Universe of unlimited supply for ALL. At a cellular and emotional level, I feared that there was not enough good to go around and our little family needed to stick together. I had not raised my sons to fit into the system of the status quo (guilt) and was responsible for their survival.

At the core of my money issues lay my issues of separation from Source. Thanks to P'Taah, I stopped asking the worn out question, "What should I *do* to support myself?"

The question became "How can I open to *allow* the Universe to support me?"

The answers were basic and I followed instructions. I consistently acknowledge the many ways the Universe supports me and that I am worthy to receive. I no longer apologize for my need to receive money for the spiritual work I do. My Sacred Work is my life and my livelihood. Gradually, I am overcoming my awkwardness in receiving payment and beginning to respond graciously and gratefully to what others give me. I have stopped arguing with loving sisters who pay more than my asking price and tender heartedly receive from those stretching their economic perimeters to pay the minimal fee. They all give back to me in special ways that touch my heart, bidding it to open to More. I have committed to evolve my money consciousness. I do not energize our dysfunctional economic system by berating it. I uphold the vision of a New Earth spiritual economy based on quality of life factors for the good of all.

Lots of repatterning material in this area! Old, old patterns of allegiance to beliefs in lack and limitation. Equating time and money and seeing them both in short supply. Holding economically prosperous people in contempt. Fearing what I hold sacred can be contaminated by money. Buying into the notion that, somehow, Spirit that moves through all things did not move through money. Believing it is more spiritually and politically *correct* to be poor. Reading the menu of life from right to left. Limiting what the Universe wants to provide me by holding onto limiting concepts of what is possible. Undermining my own vision of a New Earth with beliefs that the transformation is a financial impossibility.

The most dynamic way I shift my consciousness from beliefs in lack to plenty is to remember how temple life felt in prosperous times. I remember how we all cooperated for the good of residents of the temple and surrounding community. I remember how music, art and beauty abounded;

how having our basic needs met was an underlying principle of daily life. These were the ways of the Goddess. As a Priestess to the World, I take these memories and transfer them to life in the Temple of the Living Earth and know there is plenty for all. I acknowledge Earth as Goddess and ask her to teach me the mystery of abundance, for she is indeed adept at abundantly manifesting in this dimension. Now I am learning to allow her to teach me to harvest the abundance of my own labors.

One of the ways I am being taught is through *The Medicine Woman Inner Guidebook & Tarot Deck* by Carol Bridges. The cards speak of the indwelling consciousness in all things and Earth's eternal fertility. They call us to restore harmony with the Earth and thus with the material world and ourselves.

I am not the hardy outdoors woman I would like to be. I depend on many aspects of the *modern world* and I am in no shape to *rough it*. But I do not want to live under the spell of materialism. Separate from Earth, I am separate from the feminine mysteries that freely reveal themselves when we live in balance with Nature.

The more conscious I become, the more perfection I see in the Creation Process. I realize the value of the Goddess' underworld descent for rest and renewal. I even find merit in the ascent of patriarchy and the foundational nature of the Old Earth. And I have a lot of faith in humanity. But, I sure would like to fast forward The Process and get a sneak preview.

What I would like to get a real good look at is the future housing situation. Over the winter, I progressed in my capacity to accept the lifestyle of others, different from mine. I reached a new level of awareness that the stage setting for each person's life supported the evolution of his or her personal process. In accepting this, I was able to embrace my truth that for me to flourish, I needed housing very different from the norm. I moved again in May, anticipating it was time to have space that would function as a center and home. I was even guided to write up the following statement:

Seeking Benefactor to provide a spacious home in a beautiful private setting in Tucson, appropriate for use as a Vitalizing Center of the emerging Spiritual Earth Culture. The unoccupied space is needed by April or May for at least one year. A central location is preferred.

"Ask and ye shall receive. Seek and ye shall find."

I give thanks knowing it is done!

I signed my name and added my phone number. At first, I thought this was just an intention statement to place on my altar. Later, I felt inner prompting to make numerous copies to distribute. I argued with this guidance! Guidance chided, *C'mon, Nicole. If you want to live in a brave new World, you'd better start living life more boldly.*

I did as directed. Friends cheered me on. I got two strange phone calls and that was it. So much for being bold. But the exercise did prime the pump of my consciousness and related thoughts flowed more freely. Everything I needed would organically arise when I needed it out of my own resource-full-ness.

Moving date was nearing. I was not clear about what to do next. I did not have the money to rent a spacious home. Did I want to live in or out of town? Should I live alone or with a housemate? Would it be better to house-sit and save money? I was not getting answers to my questions and I did not like anything I saw.

Finally, I remembered that *The Celestine Prophecy* states that the Universe always has the answers to our questions, but we do not always get the questions right. My mind quickly reprogrammed and incorporated the factor of the date when I needed to vacate my current location. Question: "What is the best possible living situation for me to be in by May 4?"

The answer materialized the next day! It was very personal space. Not a center. It came close to being what I had wanted, for myself, for some time. Space defines how one conducts one's life. I do not want to live in space designed to get the dweller to consume. I want creative space that I happen to live in, not living space I try to create in. I want an environment of elegant simplicity furnished only with that which supports my Sacred Work. The little guest house that became available to me the next day was a tiny kernel of my heart's desire. It was a free standing garage conversion with potential to be attractively simple. The white brick interior, well-placed windows, and high ceiling fostered creative energies. It was a compact miniature of what I wanted. A small kitchen and bathroom. An open creating/living/sleeping area. Me space. With little time or effort, I could easily keep it clean and organized the way I need to live. This frees time and energy to enjoy life out-of-doors and to explore the many rooms of inner consciousness.

It did not harmonize with nature in ways that ignite creative fires, but it was in a pleasant, central neighborhood with large trees and abundant plant life. There was even a tiny, private yard space. I felt so sure that this was the best possible living situation for me to be in at this time, that I signed the year's lease. My gypsy self would have to settle for occasional short trips this summer. My Priestess Self needed to have a personal sanctuary and base for her expanding work in Tucson.

Verification that I needed a sanctuary, not a center, came through an astrology reading a few days after I signed the lease. In the past, I had benefited from occasional readings of my solar return, transit, and progressed charts that indicated current forces at play. However, I tend to feel only slight resonance with interpretations of my natal chart indicating lifetime forces. Friends urged me to experience Daniel Giamario's astrological wizardry, assuring me that his interpretation would be different. And it was!

Most of his work as an astrologer had focused on cracking the code of how astrology can be most useful at this particular turning of the ages. This he calls Shamanic Astrology, which takes into account the reality of where we are as a culture, a planet, and where we are in overall cycles. And it recognizes all paths as valid. Daniel believes that the Universe is supportive of human beings who consciously participate with their cycles. When one understands intent, one understands the nature of initiation that a given cycle represents and can then consciously co-create with the Great Mystery.

He also proposes that working with archetypes (the original pattern of any design) is the fastest way to have astrology work in one's life. Archetypal material gives us a sense of possibilities available and which ones apply to us. The Shamanic Astrology system deals with archetypes. It is a powerful tool for sorting out the symbols and archetypes of the past and gives clues about what the new archetypes will look like on the other side of the Turning of the Ages.

Now this I can relate to! Further, Daniel suggests that a good portion of traditional western astrology today is patriarchal and we should question its authority. He indicates that the popular practice of Sun sign identification began about 100 years ago because it is easy to determine. Over-emphasizing its importance is very limiting as it is much less individualistic than other factors on one's chart.

His shamanic interpretation, presented in ninety minutes, did more to crystallize my self-awareness than many of my efforts put together in a lifetime. He indicated that I had a rare path of subtle paradoxes - a hall of mirrors. How good it was to have what I have so often felt named. Without having any background information on me, he indicated that I was in window of time that he called the window of the Dianic Priestess. This was a virginal cycle. A Priestess point of concentrated focus on Priestess stuff and on my own space. It was an empowerment phase that began in March of 1994 and would end February of 1995. The first circle of Priestesses formed in March and would be ordained in February. How was this for synchronicity! Perhaps, the alone space intent of this Dianic cycle pre-empted having community space for a Vitalization Center.

Daniel emphasized the value of working with this cycle. He warned that a lover relationship now would be a distraction and urged me to "Turn away!" if one presented itself. This was an enormous opportunity to reclaim my sovereignty, to again become Virgin, Whole and Complete unto myself. In this consciousness of wholeness, he said I could more aptly fulfill my desire for "non-hierarchical, conscious, equal, process-oriented partnership." I asked him to repeat himself. It was a mouthful, but I had never heard my desire articulated so precisely.

He said it was right there on my chart. I had Libra Rising with my North Node in the First House. This means my life purpose issues are about "sovereign, autonomous self doing conscious partnership." These were words sent by the Goddess! Perhaps, I was not in search of the impossible dream. Perhaps, as Daniel said, it was my Life's intent to quest for what had appeared as an ever elusive partnership. "Quest and **find**," he affirmed. "But this does not mean easy partnering. It means conscious relationship is your path to God. And at this turning of the ages, it is about inventing totally new ways to be in relationship. For you, the only reason to be in relationship is when you realize you can't learn anything more about yourself on your own and need to be with someone to learn more. It's not because you're not okay on your own, because you are. It's about getting a reflection back from someone who's an equal, if not more so. If you start identifying who you are by who you're with, that's regressive and will do you in."

The Sagittarius influences explained my questing nature. My Moon (lineage), Venus (the Goddess imagery I am working with), and Mercury (how I think) were all in Sagittarius. This is the renuncient, the non-householder, the questing philosopher who dares to go where no one else has gone before in order to expand self to the widest possible horizons. Another mouthful. Further, due to the position of my south node, indications were that I had been a Sagittarian who bonded with a partner on the trail for as long as we were traveling the same way. Another crystallization. I who lived so at odds with the cultural norm, lived in harmony with the design of the Zodiac. I felt fully validated for the first time in my life. Only my Capricorn Sun Sign afforded me validation under patriarchy. This Sun fuel that I burn generates qualities of responsible management of one's domain. The astrological intent is to do so to accomplish my current life purpose. By being responsible, I survived under patriarchy. By listening and responsibly responding to the Guiding Voice Within, I found ways to live my truth and thrive.

I also felt validated to hear that, with Cancer in my Mid-Heaven place of right livelihood, it was my nature to always be part of the process. Professionals often criticized me for not keeping professional distance as a teacher or facilitator, even though they were in awe of my abilities to be both teacher and friend to students, facilitator and sister to workshop participants. The design for this lifetime is that, in whatever work I do, I am around people who have the best values of community and personal connection. As Daniel put it, "You could never be a hired gun who just goes in to get the job done."

Through the reading, I also discovered why Graham and I were so at odds. We were perfectly mismatched! Spiritual soul mates ideally mismatched in the tangible world to stimulate growth. Shamanic astrology interprets a woman's Mars position as her animus, her magical masculine, the Eros or life force energy that activates her life. It is what she is physically attracted to and where her romantic love issues lie. This does not always correspond with relationship intent, which for me is consciously working on relationship. This is about synthesizing one's Venus feminine self and one's masculine Mars self. It is the sacred inner marriage that must occur before it is possible to have it in relationship.

Venus is the anima of a man, his magical feminine. All of the above principles apply. If a man has not taken responsibility for that archetype within himself, he will project it on the women in his life, expecting them to do for him what he needs to do for himself. The same is true for a woman, in her relationships with men. She must take responsibility for her animus archetype. My Mars is in Scorpio. This is Green Man, the Horned God, the Wild Man who honors woman on her terms in wildness. Graham's Venus is in Cancer. This is the Great Mother who achieves her identity by nurturing her mate and her family. Wide-eyed, I could now clearly see our unconscious projections on each other! We could not see each other for who we were. No wonder I so often felt *not me* with Graham. No doubt, he felt the same way with me. I felt compassion for us both. Neither of us could meet the other's needs. I fortified my commitment to consciously engage the inner sacred marriage. Daniel indicated that I could do so by developing an erotic relationship with the Earth - being near waterfalls, in oak groves, in green, moist, fecund settings. This would be a challenge here in the dry desert, but there were certainly accessible, inviting places nearby to engage Green Man.

Daniel did not know about my Priestess work or my relationship to Green Man. His Venus is in Virgo and he identifies strongly with the High Priestess Archetype. He pointed out that in Tucson, my Rising Sign is in Virgo. Though one's natal chart always takes precedence over other influences, this explained why my work with the Sacred Feminine was so pronounced here. Daniel uses a Jungian definition of the *Sacred Work – when you wake up each morning knowing you are getting up to do what you were born to do, you are doing the Sacred Work*. This is so for me. And I am most grateful.

Later, Daniel worked with the charts of the first circle of Priestesses and identified the archetypes of the group. Lots of Wild Woman, vision questing, trail blazing energy here, along with High Priestess and Tantrika energies. I figured out the archetypes for the second circle. More Wild Women, Vision Questers, High Priestesses, and Tantrikas. Added were the Female Boddhisattvas, Female Avatars, Matriarchs, and Amazon Queens. These were not women's auxiliary circles formed to serve the Patriarchs! No wonder we made soul agreements to come together when it was time for us to reclaim our unique powers and purposes. No wonder I felt our collective potential was explosive.

And no wonder we feared our own power. We had no viable choice other than to bring about a new age in which the primal, earthy, root chakra powers of the Goddess were again honored and celebrated. This meant we needed to honor and celebrate those aspects in ourselves or we would wither away. Our souls were committed to work with the finer, subtle energy fields **and** to be firmly grounded. We needed to consciously and intently bring forth the New Priestess.

Several women acknowledged apprehension, even fear, that if they followed the New Priestess path, they would become like me. They would have to give up their mates, their families, their homes and lifestyles. They would be alone and devoid of belongings. Others wished they could live as I do. As the Priestess process evolved, each woman compared less and got clearer about what was right for her in relationships and lodging. Some relationships ended. Others improved greatly. And new loves were found. A few men revealed an extraordinary capacity to support their partner in embracing her fullness. All of the women discovered greater love of Self and developed greater capacity to live their lives consciously.

Most women found themselves doing inner and outer housecleaning and clearing. The New Priestess was defining her own domain to support the truth and beauty of who she is. Depressions lifted. Vision cleared. New purposes revealed themselves. Some quit jobs that drained them. Some moved to new places. Some chose solitary paths. Some found inner resources to face major health challenges with high regard for themselves and their bodies. Through tears and laughter, each awakening Priestess was reclaiming the richness of inner life and transforming outer life accordingly. Opening . . . opening . . . opening to new possibilities.

They did not always notice their rapid progression until I, as witness, called it to their attention. For a moment, they could look away from the chaos of their transformation and delight in their growth. They could let go of their conviction that all the other women had it more together and were better *qualified* to become Priestesses. Increasingly, they are aware of the vibrational quickening as they awaken, and of the unexpected and magical ways the Intentions they declared at their Initiation are being actualized. More quickly than they realized, they were claiming their truth and living it.

As the date for the first circle's ordination neared, one of the Initiates voiced dismay that she did not fit in the design. I urged her to determine what was right for her, saying, "The last thing I want is for you to force yourself into a shoe that does not fit."

She laughed and responded, "That's one thing I've really gotten from you. Which means I've been running around barefoot for nine months."

Yes, each of the Sacred Sisters has been barefoot and pregnant with herself. And the pending birthings of the New Priestesses are sure to be momentous occasions of great joy. Lily Beautiful Shield read the Akashic Records of the First Circle in their first trimester. She addressed an aspect of my service to the group. "Many . . . or all of you, are really under her . . . well, it's more than guidance. It is more like her protective wing, a cloak that is shielding many of you from being assaulted, being attacked. I don't mean literally attacked, but psychically attacked. She offers to each one of you a great deal of her personal protection and whether this is on a conscious or subconscious level, I see her enveloping each one of you with a kind of feeling or aura . . . a mist . . . around the whole group." I, who lived under the protective wing of the Goddess Isis, extended that protection until they were ready to claim it for themselves. Ready to reclaim the power of their own Divinity that is absolute protection.

As a spiritual midwife, I feel wonderfully part of their pregnancies. A statement encapsulating the nature of my work appeared in the 1994 Winter Solstice Fellowship of Isis edition of *Isian News*. The content was a distillation of a conversation one of the Initiates had with Lady Olivia during a visit to Clonegal Castle. It reads: "The Rev. Nicole Christine trains candidates for the Priesthood with sensitivity and an understanding of what being a Priestess in these days means. She treats others, not from above, but as a sister, sharing experiences, rather than just giving teachings."

Yes! Yes! This is the essence of The Process! I find no glory in being *above* others. The glory is being *among* my sisters. Through shared experiences, we see the old ways with new eyes and evolve into the new with wisdom. We come together at the Pool of our Shared Essence and bathe in the purifying waters of the Sacred Feminine. We are the Old Priestesses. We are the New Priestesses.

By looking into lives of the Priestess Past, I learned more about what the New Priestess is not. In Marion Zimmer Bradley's book *Forest House*, the High Priestess took trance inducing potions in order to deliver the oracles of the Goddess to the people. Worldly politics were gaining dominance over spiritual principles. The High Druid *interceded* and made sure the words the people heard supported his political interests. The potions were slowly poisoning the body of the High Priestess and the twisted words of the Goddess were poisoning the minds of the people.

I do not believe the New Priestess is to replicate the old ways. I believe she becomes her own Oracle and encourages others to do the same. Nor do I believe that she abdicates her own power or way of life to serve a God or Goddess outside herself or promote worship of external forces. I believe the New Priestess consciously aligns with the Archetypal Gods and Goddesses to co-create with the Great Mystery and that she intentionally embodies the highest qualities of her Goddess Self. She knows herself as Woman, Priestess, Goddess. She remembers how to see into the Invisible and bring forth into the visible what appropriately serves in this period of transformation. She holds the vision and the energy for All Life as we complete a 26,000 year cycle in our evolutionary journey through time and space. She does so conscious of the oneness of the darkness and the light, death and rebirth. She does so with the consciousness that preparing a meal, partaking of it, cleaning up afterward and taking out the garbage is as much a sacred ritual as preparing a ceremony, taking communion, and being sure the ceremonial ground is in as good or better shape after the ceremony as it was when she entered it.

Centered in a rich inner life, the New Priestess learns to walk in beauty and balance, magnifying the energy of the Temple of the Living Earth. She learns and uses Gaia's language. She lives in heartfelt communion with the Divine. By consciously embracing life with focused intention and attentive, guided response to synchronistic flows, she is not dependent on amulets, formulas, mantras, or spells to connect with Source. As a Priestess to the World, she does not see herself above or apart from others or consider her spiritual life and her worldly life as separate. She knows there is a Priestess in every woman and a Priest in every man who holds all life as sacred. She honors her process and the process of others.

Discovering the qualities of the New Priestess entails discovering the qualities of the new woman. The book *I Sit Listening To The Wind* by Judith Duerk expands the quest for wholeness by exploring the Inner Masculine. Through prose, poetry, and reflective questions, she gracefully reveals what it means to be enlivened or to be dominated by one's animus. A balance is struck between the masculine urge to DO and the feminine need to BE.

A Woman's Worth by Marianne Williamson discusses how the reemergence of women will heal the world. I do not want to wound or be wounded any more. I believe there is more to life than warring and healing, only to war again. I believe that activation of our Creative Life Force is the best way to prevent wars and to heal. By holding sacred space for everyone to come into his or her greatness, we will co-create a reality surpassing our wildest present day imaginings.

The next step in The Process is to open to the involvement of men. A book, entitled *To All The Men I've Loved*, is waiting inside me to be written. It pays tribute to the men who have influenced my development through joy and sorrow and uplifts an evolved view of the Sacred Masculine. It begins with my father and includes my brothers, sons, husbands, lovers, and friends. The shadow and bright sides of sexual and emotional relationships will be openly explored. The final pages are to be written by Green Man Priests aligning with this archetype to renew our lost unity with the Natural Realm.

A healing essential to my evolution occurred when I was able to acknowledge the Green Man aspect of Graham. His response to my action of releasing my interests in VisionPoint felt like a slap in the face. Old wounds reopened. Doors to financial remuneration closed. Our relationship was bad for my health. Ensuing limited contact always confirmed this. Through mutual friends and his writings, I learned he now felt strongly connected to the Goddess. I had no comment. We were each evolving in our own time and way and our time together was finished.

On rare occasions, I returned to VisionPoint. She calls to me often and always welcomes me as her closest friend. Our reunion renews my body and spirit in ways nothing else can. Just prior to quit-claiming the land to Graham, I went into a rage when I discovered red brick landscaping borders constructed by him. I was appalled that he would impose this *Home Depot vibration* on the land! If he had to use something, why not native rocks or adobe bricks in colors that harmonized with the tan Earth! What a violation of me and the land! I tore his work apart with a vengeance and piled the bricks aside. Simultaneously, I felt better and worse. I freed the land and imprisoned myself deeper into internal conflict with Graham.

Neither of us mentioned my action. When I returned in September 1994, he was there, as were even more red brick walls. Graham's welcome was warm. Our conversation limited. I walked the land I so love, absorbing its love for me. I was grateful that much of it remained undisturbed. I did not like the changes Graham was making, but found myself accepting his creative process with VisionPoint. This man was born in Detroit. He had been a developer and left that behind, now living off real estate investments. In search of land to purchase, he found his way to the mountain and he, too, loves, and is loved by, this land. He was finding his way to renew his lost unity with the Natural Realm. VisionPoint could absorb the *Home Depot vibration*. And I would always hold VisionPoint sacred no matter what *develops*. I was remembering that all the Earth, all Life, is sacred whether in the city or countryside, at a shopping mall or a hidden grove. Furthermore, by working with him to revitalize investment properties, I had acquired funds in our divorce that were financing my Sacred Work. For this and the wisdom gleaned from the hard lessons of our relationship, I am most grateful.

A wave of inner peace gently moved through me. I had not been able to ward off the wave of white invaders in my indigenous lifetimes. I had not been able to hold back the wave of consumerism and land development. I do not understand people who are enamored by machines and war. I cannot comprehend rape and scrape consciousness. But I do believe in the invincibility of Spirit and that there is a greater Design to all of this, a bigger picture. And I can feel the tides turning, and delight in knowing they cannot be held back. Our ancient ancestors upheld the belief that we belong to the Earth. Modern thought has been that the Earth belongs to us. Green Man's return reminds us of our Oneness with All Life. He helps us see that by exploiting Gaia, we exploit ourselves and that, conversely, by loving and caring for Her, we love and care for ourselves.

There is much talk of the end of the world. Yes, the end of the world as we have known it is coming and I rejoice in this apocalypse. Only those who fear the transformation will go through it *grating and gnashing* their teeth. I have learned to redirect my rage to seek creative resolutions and harness the adrenaline rush of fear for the Greater Good. I intend to go through these changing times smiling, hand in hand with every man, woman, and child ready to seed a New Earth with the consciousness that we are one with each other and the universe. Pied Pipers of Love. Destination point: the Fifth World of Peace and Illumination.

Men have been wounded under patriarchal and matriarchal systems. The men's movement bears testimony to the way men also benefit by having safe space in which to heal and bring forth their True Selves. I experienced healings of my inner masculine hearing men in the New Warrior movement intimately share their process of healing their maleness and their inner femaleness. I felt safer truly being a woman. This gives me great hope. As women reclaim the Sacred Feminine Mysteries and men reclaim the Sacred Masculine Mysteries, we can attune to the Mysteries of Woman and Man,

Goddess and God. Then we can learn from one another in ways that foster healthy mothering of sons and fathering of daughters and evolving all our relationships. It is only when women and men come together authentically that we can begin to define true partnerships as friends, lovers, mates. We are sexual/spiritual beings. Only when women and men, whatever their sexual preferences, are empowered can we lovingly, joyfully, naturally channel the creative sexual life force and co-create a Celestial Earth society.

The truth of these times is not about bringing back matriarchy. It is not about blaming the patriarchs for what has or has not occurred. It is about redefining what we deify, what we hold sacred. For me, it is not about worshipping a sky god of benevolent or vengeful intent or a nurturing or destructive Earth goddess. It is about ceasing the religious practice of worshipping false images in ourselves and others, and seeing the God and Goddess in every man and woman and the Divinity in every season, cycle, and circumstance. It is dancing to mend the Sacred Hoop of the Nations. It is co-creating and celebrating the life force that courses through our bodies when we are open to the aliveness of All Life. The Earth is alive. The trees. The animals. The rocks. The waters. The fire and air. How alive are we?

ॐ

My personal truth was evolving and I was making peace with these times. In one moment of rhythmic aliveness, my issues with technology dissolved and I was no longer in conflict with my whiteness. The sacred hoop of my soul mended. I was at the Fourth Avenue Street Fair dancing to pipe and percussion sounds of an indigenous musical group from the Andes. The obvious gently permeated my consciousness. This group would not be here for me to enjoy were it not for technology. They would not have the acoustical sound system or the capacity to sell their CDs, anymore than I could be writing of this, were it not for technology. Mind, machines, materialism and money made this possible. These forces were linking up the people of the Heart, the Mind, the Body, and Spirit. Soon we would remember that we are One People, One Planet.

The more I focus on Oneness, I discover more Oneness to focus upon. By dispelling my beliefs in separation, I consciously engage a holographic Universe and simultaneous time. Once I perceived memories of other lives in terms of past life recall. Now I experience the Now of all my lives. The same white woman who identifies as a New Priestess embodying the Goddess is a Tibetan Monk taking refuge in the Buddha. She is a red woman in traditional buckskin silently walking in harmony with the Earth and her Chippawa mate whom Nicole divorced sixteen years ago. She is an armed black youth fighting with his people to end apartheid in South Africa. S/he is all this and so much more. We are all so much more than we allow ourselves to remember.

I ask myself, how much am I willing to remember? How expansive will I let myself become? How alive do I dare to be? Am I willing to resolve my inner conflict to truly experience external peace and harmony? Am I truly ready to publicly profess such transformational shifts in consciousness? Have I evolved enough as a white woman with incredible opportunities to develop my mind, to use it to harmonize the Feminine and Masculine aspects of Mind for the Greatest Good for All? Do I really intend to co-create a New Earth? Do I even honestly believe it is possible?

28

My questions were answered on my birthday, December 26, 1994, in an astrology reading for 1995. This one was delightfully done by Carolyn Brent, writing collaborator and student of Daniel Giamario. In sharp contrast to 1993, ALL SYSTEMS ARE GO! Universal forces support the emergence of the writer, public reception of the vision, manifestation of resources, travel, and higher levels of relatedness with others. It is prime time for a conscious love partnership. I stayed up late that night to celebrate the exact moment of my birth and affirm my intention to fully and consciously participate with these cycles. At 11:45 p.m., I spontaneously began jumping up and down shouting *YES! YES! YES! My time is NOW!*

Earlier that day, I read a birthday card from a beloved High Priestess Sister. It bore this message. . .

Dearest Nicole,

A child has been born during a sacred time and it is appropriate to give thanks to the Goddess, our Great Earth Mother, and the Guardians of the Four Sacred Directions. She is to be an enlightened one, a teacher of all that is special and sacred and truly pure, not tainted by the Christian Priests and local authorities looking to control the people, especially the powerfully gifted women. This child is to be a Priestess and she will serve to protect and keep all that is truly sacred and balanced. Her name is Nicole Christine and she will be raised in secrecy. But, oh, there is so much joy for her birth!

Thank you for being born, Sister Nicole! High Priestess! Believe in the magic of your birth! You are a gift!

I Love You!
Debbie

At first, it was difficult for me to even read these words, much less receive the love and appreciation they contain. I put the card aside until I could come back to it with an open heart. As I read, I cried with gratitude. My life is no longer a secret. I have been found out. Found out by my

Sacred Sisters. We have found each other and found ourselves. And in so doing we found the Goddess.

The day before, I heard the words, "Those who listen and follow their Inner Voice either go insane or become a legend." [18] I have listened and followed my Inner Voice, often fearing it was taking me to the brink of insanity, even though it always moves me through delusion and darkness into lucidity and light. I have not always believed the Voice, and I certainly have not entertained the idea of becoming a legend. But these are legendary times alive with personal myths. Times when more are listening and following their Inner Voice. We do not all hear the same words. We are not all guided down the same path or through the same process. But we are all Living Legends. The One and the Many always becoming More.

≈

I had a strange revelation writing these final pages on The Process. Strange in the sense that I did not realize the obvious till now. Writing was becoming a struggle. So many pieces of the puzzle to put in place. So many loose ends to weave into the tapestry. This was taking more time than I had allotted.

Beyond the personal benefit of integrating aspects of my own process, did it really matter if I had a finished product or not? In the grand scheme of things, it does not matter if I keep writing, if I live my vision, if I do anything at all. The more I know about myself, the more I realize that I am not motivated by love or money, by recognition or the approval of others; or by adventure or self-satisfaction. I am not even motivated by a desire for good to triumph over evil, right over wrong, because I no longer embrace the world of duality. I know myself as a speck of cosmic dust and as the Cosmos Itself.

I can stop writing, stop Priestessing, stop trying to find a hearth that fires my Creative Flame. I can even stop eating, and Life will continue. Then what is the inner force compelling me to keep writing and striving for a brave new world? I sat with the feelings of this inner force and this compulsion, sinking into the consciousness of these energy flows. In the Stillness, I felt a deep pulsing, a throbbing at the core of my being. This is the impulse to create! All existence rises out of this pulsing vibration. The compelling inner force is the cosmic urge to create!

I reconnected to the center of the Universe! I felt the heartbeat of Creation, saw this glowing ember of creative energy. This is Goddess-Realization! By vibrating with the Creative Pulse, the Gods and Goddesses create their universes. All my compulsions to repattern, clear the past, heal my wounds and make amends, rise out of a primal need to keep the Creative Channels open. All my intensive inner work to develop powers of focused concentration, to be in right relationship with people, money, my environment, my body, is done to maximize my capacity to create. All my starts and stops with marriages, careers, living situations, have been experiential workshops on creativity. All the betrayals and disappointments have made me wise, and inspired me to create a better world. My world is a panoramic landscape of my spirit's insatiable desire to create. The Voice I respond to as Guidance, is the Voice of my Creative Self seeking ever expanding avenues of expression.

Part of the strangeness of this realization is that I felt so blah about it. Absent was any of the exhilaration I normally get from a major aha!. Sitting with the *blahness*, I discovered that it is *ego deflation*. Ego has been exposed. It is not the Creator. It was created by the Creator to bring creations into worlds. The blahness will dissolve once my consciousness realigns to incorporate and activate these shifts in awareness. By consciously aiming beyond my highest expectations within the old paradigm, I can transcend ego boundaries and enter the new paradigm of my own creation. Then my personality will know it has more magnificent creations to uniquely express. This process may take weeks, even years, but when it is complete, I will experience the exhilarating explosion of greater clarity. My subconscious, conscious, and superconscious fields will be realigned and my creative powers will expand exponentially. Then I will be able to sit, to throb with the Creative Pulse. Then I will be in position to truly co-create a New Reality.

To the Creative Process, I offer this work. To the Creative Process, I commend my spirit. To the Creative Process, I give my thanks.

The Priestess

On February 2, 1995, in a candlelit house in a beautiful desert setting, seven women ceremonially awakened their Priestess Selves. It was the evening of Candlemas, St. Brigit's Day, when this Goddess of the Triple Flame is honored. A time of purification, rebirth, and rekindling of the inner fire. A time of dedication to the Goddess. In the original circle of ten Initiates, one moved away and two chose solitary paths. Each woman determined her own state of readiness and calling according to her unique relationship with the Goddess. My role was to be sure we were in harmony with one another and energetically aligned with the Intention of the Ceremony.

We did not fully realize what this Circle of Trailblazers was birthing until their last gathering as Initiates. The nine month gestation period was nearly ended. It was time to finalize preparations for the ordination ceremony. Mary wanted to be ordained in the Fellowship of Isis. Makala would proclaim herself a Priestess to the World in the Temple of the Living Earth. Sharon, Linda, and Sereena would do both. Victoria had decided she was not ready to do either. Cynthia was at home sick and we were not sure of her decision.

We had enough pieces to put our ceremonial puzzle together. Our location was set. Guests had been invited. Each Initiate was determining her ceremonial garb that would express her own uniqueness. The second Circle of Initiates would serve as handmaidens by handling room setup and feast arrangements. We began to co-create the ceremony, experimentally enacting it as we went along. The Process Design portrays association with the Fellowship of Isis as a linking with the Mysteries of the Great Goddess of 10,000 faces. Alignment with the Temple of the Living Earth thoughtform energizes planetary awakening and Gaia's evolution into Celestial Earth consciousness. To be connected to both, bridges the Old and the New. Soon it was evident that Mary, choosing to solely be ordained in the lineage of Isis, was our anchor in the Old Earth. Makala, the anchor in the New. Linda, Sharon, and Sereena formed the bridge between the two worlds! Our soul commitment of long ago was now fulfilled!

A trail had been blazed from the plundered temple of our long ago past to our now. The journey had been arduous, but we had arrived and fortified ourselves through the renewal of our Sisterhood. We stood at the chasm between the Old World and the New. Mary, with her love for druidry and witchery, opened her scroll and evoked the ancient ways when the people loved and worshipped the land. And we remembered. Makala, exhausted by her journey, needed virgin soil. Her scroll led her to the New Earth where we joined her. The other women were to carry the teachings of their scrolls forth into the New Earth. They were a bridge on which others yet to come might cross. Between them, these awakened women were remembering how to live and honor their truth and the truth of their sisters, to embrace the shadow and the light, heal through touch, inspire through breath, bring forth life and honor the blood mysteries, respect death, reclaim the sacred erotic, evolve the old ways and birth the new, unify the feminine and the masculine, and joyfully celebrate themselves, Life, Nature, and Celestial Earth. Their awakened consciousness would serve the people of the New Earth well.

We had two weeks to go and much to prepare, inwardly and outwardly. The act of simply making it to the ordination proved to be a feat of bringing Heaven and Earth together. We did not have a temple to retreat to. We all experienced many worldly distractions. Our commitment to *Earth our spirituality* was tested again and again. And we each tapped into our vast Inner Resources and passed again and again.

Within a few days, Victoria called to say she was feeling separate and incomplete about her decision not to take the final step. We talked about her apprehensions and feelings of inadequacy. She is the eldest and cancer revealed itself as her Teacher early in the Awakening Process. We were all committed to her well being. The Healing Ritual and group Reiki treatments we had done on her behalf deepened our bonds with one another and I expressed the sadness we felt without her. Beyond that, it was up to her to know within herself what was right for her. Three days prior to the ceremony, she called and said, "I am ready." Tears filled my eyes and I gave thanks. I, too, felt incomplete by her decision not to go the distance with us after we had come so far together. She and Cynthia would proclaim themselves Priestesses to the World. Makala would anchor the New Earth energies. Victoria and Cynthia would help establish the new.

Tears increasingly flowed as the ceremony neared. So much had transpired in so little time. Not only was there a Priestess Sisterhood, there was a growing feeling of community. Initiates were co-creating a Spring Equinox Celebration to honor the many daughters among us in the season of the maiden. The next night, Priestesses and Initiates from the North and the

South would answer Leah's call to help hold the energy for a community celebration of hundreds in Sedona. Men, aligning with Green Man consciousness, were emerging. We reclaimed April Fool's Day as Green Man Day and plans were in the making for an April 1 potluck, an honoring ritual for men, and a Talking Circle to discuss community building. Several men were making Green Man masks and costumes for our Earth Day celebration later in April. Sixteen women were creating a Praises to Gaia Sacred Dance Ritual for that day that will also include an Earth-honoring dance performance by the children. Exponential expansion would be energized at the Ordination because the New Priestesses were ready and eager to give their gifts and take on part of my work. And I was ready to activate the next phases of the Divine Design.

So often I had cried because community and celebration were so absent in my life. Now I cried with relief and gratitude for its organic emergence. My role as an initiator was not at all altruistic. Nor were my actions consciously deliberate. The yearning in my soul was simply so intense that it called loudly to others whose souls yearn for the same. Our motives in co-creating a new reality are very personal and very real. A new way of being was finding expression through us. As we broke free of the casings of the old ways, we established new ground where we and others who cared to join us could begin anew.

The closer we got to the ceremonial date, the amps were being upped for all of us in preparation for channeling the Priestess vibration and the higher octave of New Earth energies. We were all fragments of the Priestess Oversoul readying to merge into a more unified field of consciousness. I had been running increasing amounts of energy as a channel of these vibrational flows. My inner training had helped me become, as Medicine Man Fool's Crow put it, a "little hollow bone" through which Spirit could freely move and express. And my own Priestess Self kept the Goddess that I AM and the woman that I am in alignment. But when tensions erupted between Initiates in the Second Circle, I suddenly felt depleted. Preparation for and facilitation of the Ceremony required a tremendous amount of focused concentration. The conflict zapped my concentration powers. I felt so tiny and alone lying in bed that night. My body conduit was too small and worn to run the amount of energy needed to keep The Process going. My consciousness was not developed enough to hold the Immaculate Concept of this Vision. Emotional release came quietly, without sobs, and I bathed myself and my bed in the healing waters of my tears.

I slept well, but still felt depleted in the morning. That afternoon, I shared my feelings with one of the Second Circle Initiates. She offered immediate support and set a phone tree in motion urging the Initiates in that Circle to send me support and to focus on holding energy for the ceremony just three nights away. I am very sensitive to any tears in the fabric of the Sisterhood and the fabric of Life. Correspondingly, I immediately felt the mending and healing support. The conflict was part of The Process. Without it, I would not have asked for or opened to receive the regenerating powers of focused concentration from my Sisters. My spirit was renewed. I was not small and alone.

Emotional fullness flowed through me on the day of the Ordination. I was beginning to grasp the mythological magnitude of bringing into form through ceremony what had been held in consciousness for so long. I started the day with a chiropractic treatment so my body was in proper alignment to channel energies. Then I visited the DeGrazia Foundation Chapel of Our Lady of Guadalupe where the Initiations took place. Prior to the Ordination, each First Circle Initiate was to place a seven day votive candle on this altar to thank Our Lady for lighting our way. I cried, adding my candle to theirs. I cried because Sereena's husband had driven way across town to bring her candle because she was too sick to do so herself. I cried as I said to the Lady, *Your Daughters have returned and we are not alone.*

I cried as I felt her loving embrace and her response. You are my Beloved Daughters in whom I am most pleased.

One of our greatest fears in committing to the Goddess was that we would have to give up our friends and loved ones. But that was the old way. There were times in our busy lives when we fantasized about a blissful cloistered life, but now we were Priestesses in and to the World. The Earth was our Living Temple. I visited DeGrazia's grave near the chapel and thanked the artist for all he had done to co-create with nature and spirit and for making these grounds open to the public. I wandered about the gallery courtyard and threw four pennies in the Deer Dancer fountain, calling on the spirit of the deer to travel with us in the New Earth. Spotting a weather worn penny on the ground, I thought of all the souls who felt they just could not make it back to the Pool of Sacred Essence. I picked it up and tenderly tossed it in the water.

It was an incredibly perfect day. The sun was bright. The air was warm. The vegetation vibrantly green. I gave thanks to the Spirit of Tucson and the many natural places where we gathered in ritual and communion. I connected with the Spirit of Place at the public park west of town where we would gather that night. All of the nature kingdom eagerly anticipated our presence. I bowed to the Four Directions and the Four Mountain ranges that cradle our town. I felt blessed. So very blessed.

Driving home, I was startled to see a magnificent saguaro strapped to the back of a truck. Her arms were stretched to the sky and exposed feet lost dirt as the truck bumped along River Road. I could hear her trying to comfort her little ones strapped down beside her. Traffic rushed by. No one came to her aid. Telepathically, I called out to her. *I feel your plight, my sister. Hold on. You are being transplanted. I know this is hard, but at least you are not being plowed down. The two-leggeds are starting to wake up. Once enough of us begin to feel again, life will be different for all. We will feel your pain because what is done to you, we do to ourselves. We will stop harming ourselves and you. I place you on the altar of my consciousness. Be with us in spirit tonight as we dedicate ourselves to the Earth and All Our Relations.*

She called back her thanks as the truck sped further to the East. I turned my attention back toward the center of town that I call home. I had a few hours left to take care of remaining details, rest, and eat. I had packed needed paraphernalia the day before, but I wanted to take something representing Joel and Todd. Something to place on the side altar to be energized by the ceremony. I chose a water coloring by Todd that his Artist Self might finally find expression, but I could not choose something for Joel. My eyes rested on an orange Viking glass vase he had given me when he was eleven. It represented one of the many ways I had wounded him. Just as my father had gotten upset when my brothers or I gave him something, I got upset when my sons gifted me. Growing up, I thought my father's reactions were about money - or the lack of it. But in the early stages of my own awakening, I realized that neither he nor I knew how to receive. This needed to change so love could flow between us all! I hurried off to Reay's Market and purchased four bright sunflowers for the vase. I infused them with the prayer that my sons' spirits might flower in the New Earth and the balance of giving and receiving be renewed.

ॐ

I wondered if I would cry all through the ceremony. But I felt composed and clear as I stood in the candlelit room prepared to greet the Second Circle Initiates and the family and friends of the First Circle Candidates. These Sacred Sisters were centering themselves on the patio outside. I knew they would be in a circle gently rocking as we innately did when we joined together. The starlit night was filled with the magic of the desert and of Candlemas. I welcomed everyone, then said, "I particularly thank the men for being here. If your partners have had trouble explaining what they have been up to for the past nine months, it is because we have been on a journey back to Self. It has been a process of discovery for us all. My role has not been to teach them what I know, but assist them in tapping into their own inner wisdom. As women, our journey to Self requires that we reclaim the Sacred Feminine Principle, then merge with a redefined Sacred Masculine Principle in a Sacred Inner Marriage. From this space in consciousness we can experience the quality of relationships we want with others.

"To do this, we look to the ways and symbols of the Goddess to find mirrors of our Divinity as women. We are not starting a new religion or trying to re-establish old ones. We are not worshipping Deities outside ourselves. When we align with a Goddess, we are aligning with qualities that she represents, qualities that we want to embody. I believe there is a Priestess and a Priest in each of us. This is the aspect of Self that knows that all life is sacred. The Priestess aligns the woman with her Goddess Self. The Priest aligns the man with his God Self. Tonight you will witness seven women acknowledging themselves as Priestesses. This is not an exclusionary act, for in so doing, we are honoring the Priest and the Priestess within each of you."

I then gave a brief overview of the ceremony and asked the men who were willing to be processional Guardians at the Gate to take strategic positions. I had cried during the day thinking about this, so grateful knowing they were willing to do so. So grateful to have the hearth protected by Masculine energies so that we could surrender deeply into the energy force field of the Feminine. I did not cry now, but I felt even more grateful to actually see them stand in support of us. When they took their positions, Gina, from the Second Circle began drumming the heartbeat on her large Tarahumara drum.

With everything prepared in the ceremonial space, I joined the Priestess Candidates on the patio. They were swaying together and gently laughing. We had laughed and cried a lot during the nine months that passed by so quickly. It felt wonderful to join them in the circle. Looking at them, I again felt the mystery of their transformations. Their radiant faces indicated they were ready, but I needed to hear them state as much. I named each woman and asked if she was ready and willing to be ordained as a Priestess in the Fellowship of Isis and/or proclaim herself a Priestess to the World in the Temple of the Living Earth. Not one woman wavered in her affirmative response. So Be It. So Be It.

❧

The eight of us approached the glowing fireplace altar. We were accompanied by Ana, an ordained Fellowship of Isis Priestess and Bridget, a self-proclaimed Priestess to the World. We were a rainbow of colors. Our pathway was secured by men conscious and caring enough to stand guard while the Sacred Feminine gave birth. At the altar, we centered our being in the Sacredness of the Moment. I stepped forth and lit the red center candle to re-ignite the mystical powers of the Life Giving Blood Mysteries. I then lit a white votive candle, offering my light to the New Priestesses. We turned to form a circle with every one and gave thanks for the Presence of the Visible and Invisible Ones. The unifying Presence of Isis and Osiris from the Heavenly Realms and Gaia and Green Man from the Earthly Realms was acknowledged along with the Gods and Goddesses revered by the Priestesses. Present among us were Ishtar, Tara, Cerridwen, Artemis, Diana, the Druids of old, Kwan Yin, Brigid, Bast, Dana, Tonancin, Our Lady of Guadalupe/Tonantzin, Kali, Mary, White Buffalo Woman, Jesus, Archangel Michael, Lakshmi, the Goddesses of Joy and Laughter and of Love and Compassion, and the Ancient Ones. Guests returned to their seats. A bell rang. The ceremony began.

I spoke of the legacy of the International Fellowship of Isis and of the genesis/gene of Isis from which all present came.[19] I asserted that what was occurring this night was part of the regenesis taking place on this planet as we return to the flow of ISness. Mary stepped forth to anchor the energies of the ancient ways. We faced each other and I acknowledged her as a Great Being whom I have known throughout time. I asked her to speak what was in her heart. She named the Goddesses she chose to align with as a Priestess and her eyes sparkled as she spoke of her commitment to bring forward the ways of old when the people honored the Earth and believed in magic. Then she placed a gift on the altar symbolizing her Sacred Work and lit a white candle representing the purity of her light and intention. As in ancient Egyptian times when the Priests and Priestesses were consecrated with Kyphi Oil, I anointed her chakras to activate the vibrational field of the Priestess. Now she and all she held dear were forever under the protective Wings of Isis. We embraced as Priestesses. Then Mary was lovingly received by Ana into the community of Priests and Priestesses in the Fellowship. The procedure was repeated as the others tearfully stepped forward to join the ranks of this sacred lineage. Sharon, who remembers the Design and creatively adorns herself as the Priestess of Isis that she is. Linda, who loves Gaia with all her being and is the heartbeat of her family and community. Sereena, who leads with her heart in bringing Heaven and Earth together in joy and laughter as she, too, opens to receive. Each of these women was a jewel in the spiritual crown of the Priestess Oversoul.

The love and regard we had for one another was beautifully evident. By honoring ourselves and one another, we honored the Goddess. Her Presence shown forth in these radiant faces. Now that we had paid homage to the sacredness of what has been and its essential foundational value for what is coming, we were ready to turn toward the New Earth. Makala took her position to anchor the new energies. I honored her for facing and moving through many fears that would have imprisoned her in a limiting world. She spoke of the vision in her heart, placed her gift on the altar, and lit the sixth candle. I held a basket of soil on which she placed her hands and proclaimed herself a Priestess to the World in the Temple of the Living Earth. We embraced as Priestesses of Gaia. She was followed by Victoria who, filled with love and compassion for All Life, committed to being the New Earth Keeper of the Hearth. Then Cynthia, who had midwifed many holy births for countless women, birthed her Priestess Self and committed to be guardian of the Blood Mysteries that life might emerge in sacred ways in the New Earth. Sereena, Linda, Sharon made their self-proclamations and, in body and in consciousness, formed a Sacred Bridge between the Old Earth and the New. All were warmly received into the Priestesses to the World Sisterhood by Bridget.

I sealed their proclamations with this declaration: You are Celestial Earth. Your bodies are illumined and you are One with Heaven and Earth. Give freely of your True Selves for the Greatest Good of All. And in pure acts of devotion co-creatively construct a New Earth Fulfilled in Beauty and Harmony with All That Is. It Is Done and It Is So. And All Creation gives Thanks!

With water from the Druid well at Clonegal Castle, Enniscorthy, Ireland, Mary Initiated the blessing of the Bridge. Then, each Priestess took seeds from her medicine pouch representing what she intends to sow in the New

Earth. She entrusted each of her Priestess Sisters with a seed for their pouches that her gifts might be spread far and wide. I offered each Priestess a sunflower seed infused with the Divine Design of the New Earth Fulfilled. Linda then read these words written by Dawna Markova. . .

I will not die an unlived life.

I will not live in fear

of falling or catching fire.

I choose to inhabit my days,

to allow my living to open me,

to make me less afraid,

more accessible,

to loosen my heart

until it becomes a wing,

a torch, a promise.

I choose to risk my significance

to live

so that which came to me as seed

goes to the next as blossom

and that which came

to me as blossom,

goes on as fruit.

Guests were invited to join us in a closing Circle. Sunflower seeds were offered to those wishing to help seed the New Earth. Thanks were given to all — seen and unseen. There was great cause for celebration. The Priestess had awakened!

I stayed after everyone was gone to sweep the kitchen floor and scour the bathroom sink. The handmaidens had done a fine job of cleaning up after the feast and putting the house back in order. I wanted to be sure to get the cleaning deposit back from the park system and to be sure that our ceremonial space was left in excellent condition. The little house was happy and so was I. I thanked the Spirits of Place and turned out the lights. I smiled noting that the space glowed in the dark.

It was nearly midnight when I arrived home. I unloaded the White Buffalo and put everything away. I slipped out of my green velvet ceremonial robe and into my sleeping sweats. Not so long ago, I would have felt at least a tinge of resentment about the work load I have in this lifetime, but tonight was wonderfully different. I felt blessed that I had engaged the totality of the experience. By simply being present each moment, every thought or action was whole and complete unto itself. Every moment, every thing, felt alive and sacred. This is what it means to be a Priestess to the World.

The energy coursing through my body was at a high velocity and I felt like a perfect conduit for it. I knew my usual tricks to bring myself down so I could sleep would not work. Neither reading, writing, dancing, nor eating would slow the speed. If I wanted to sleep I would have to do so at this higher vibration because it had firmly established itself. I called sleep to me that I might journey to the Dreamtime where the Celebration of the Awakened Priestesses continued.

I woke up the next morning in the New Earth. Everything looked and felt different. Less dense. More alive. Practical matters still required attention, but felt less tedious. Guidance was to work on my taxes without resisting them. I was quite surprised at how low my Priestessing income had been in 1994 and how high my Priestessing expenses were. Combining my savings and my projected Priestessing income, it looked like I would have enough to live on through the end of 1995. From an Old Earth perspective, this is not a pretty picture for a woman who will be 55 in December . . . who began working at age 10, yet has no job security, investments, retirement plans, or relatives of means to will, give, or loan her money . . . and who has done all the marrying she is going to do. Admittedly, I felt a little stomach queasiness, but I had been in much worse economic situations with much less conviction that the best is yet to come. And there is such perfection in my situation. I am highly motivated to explore New Earth economics because I am not attracted to the things money buys in the Old Earth and do not have access to "old money" by birth or circumstance. I am drawn to quality of life factors and have become the wealthiest person I know in terms of people and experiences. I have a rich inner life and have everything I need to have in the material world when I need to have it. I am learning to be receptive to all that life offers me. I am one with Heaven and Earth.

❧

I reflected on my relationship to time and money. How can I continue my work in more resourceful ways. Where am I too conservative? Where am I overly optimistic? Once clear in my intentions, I wrote them down:

I, Nicole Christine, joyfully intend to consciously and responsibly utilize my resources to seed the New Earth in 1995. I intend to fulfill my commitment to establish the four foundational Priestess Circles as anchoring cornerstones for the Ceremonial Tent which, when in place, symbolically establishes the Celestial Earth matrix of the Priestess Sisterhood. I further intend to more fully activate Gaia and Green Man consciousness, to celebrate Life, and birth Earth Song Publications through self-publication of The Temple of the Living Earth. This will prepare the way for publication of collective writings of the Awakened Priestesses. I open to receive the Greatest Good that I might have more to give and more to receive. It is done and in accordance to Divine Design and Divine Timing. And I give thanks.

When I finished writing this statement, I knew I had transcended Old Earth fears and beliefs in lack and limitation. By changing my picture of reality, the Universe could now rearrange my world to reflect my ever evolving consciousness. No fear, pain, anger, shame, blame or guilt can hold me back any longer. By linking in imagination with others, the Celestial Earth that I could not create alone was now obtainable. The spirit of the wolf, of virginal forests and sparkling rivers has returned. I feel calm, clear, and content. I feel consciously present in my own reality of sensual beauty, rampant kindness, and joyful connection to the Sacredness of All Life. I graduated. I descended deeply, bringing spirit into matter, then ascended, taking it all with me into a higher octave of consciousness. My Earthwalk has become a celebration of All That Is and a song of eternal gratitude.

Life ordained me Crystal Priestess of Gaia.

The Priest

I relate to Shamanic Astrology as an aid in living my life more consciously, not as fortune telling. I take responsibility for determining if what an astrologer tells me is written in the stars is so for me. I felt resonating elation over the possibilities my birthday reading presented. Greater opportunities to share my writings. Perhaps, after numerous publishing delays, *My Ascension Journal* would finally be released. Perhaps, I would be able to expand my sharing of the *Temple of the Living Earth* vision. More resources to bring the vision into form. Chances to roam *and* have a temple home as a gypsy Priestess. And I eagerly embraced the prospect of more evolved relationships — at least in the greater sense of community. Although, my natal chart indicates that conscious equal partnership with a mate is inevitable, and my progressed and transit charts indicate the time can be now, I found myself questioning the stars. I know I could not have held the focus for the Priestess Process *and* the focus for a primary love relationship. My life had to be organized to put the Sisterhood first. I have embraced the Dianic Priestess phase and it has served the Sisterhood and me well. The Process is in place. The story has been told. Its written form is a demonstration of my ordination commitment to use my writing skills to co-create with Gaia. Can I now *have it all* as I profess is possible? Is this even what I truly want?

I could not have made the personal progress I have made without my Sacred Sisters. I am secure in the sacredness of the Feminine Principle and do not fear depleting my energy in a lover relationship as I have in the past. I have reclaimed my virginity, my wholeness, and will never again lose it to another. Now in conscious relationship to life, I am able to choose wholeness in relationship. I know I need to bond with Sacred Brothers and feel secure in the sanctity of the Masculine Principle to actualize this wholeness; but, at the time of the reading, I felt no incentive to create space in my fulfilling life for a partner. However, an unforeseen long distance reconnection with a bygone lover created a heart opening. Even though the reconnect seems to be more about completing our past rather than moving into a future together, our communication is igniting a spark in me that had all but gone out. Lance always saw the fire in my eyes and knew how to touch the passion in my body and my soul. He could speak to the core of my being because he spoke from the core of his. Even when we were at odds, he was my staunchest ally – and still is. He is a Green Man, living in the green, moist, fecund realms of the Northwest, who knows how to honor a woman on her terms in her wildness. Domesticated though our lives look, we celebrate the untamed aspects of ourselves and each other. Neither time, space, or circumstance diminished our bond because of our ultimate trust in the Essence of the other.

Lance was a brave warrior who did battle against those who forced all the young men into wars of greed and profit. Political in his outrage against social injustices, he passionately propagandized for a communally caring world. And we loved each other for our public daring and for our personal vulnerability. But as women he loved fell wounded and dying, he put politics aside to help in their healing and their passing. He turned to a Twelve-Step circle to heal his own wounds. Then took the thirteenth step of joining a brotherhood of men defining their own sense of manliness. Now quietly spiritual, he ministers to a hospice community of souls transitioning into another world. He is a Priest to the Worlds, awakened in his own time and his own way.

This opportunity to look back in time, is providing me with an expanded perspective on my own progression and awakening. More significantly, reconnecting with Lance, who exudes the magical masculine energies of my animus, has meant a deeper reunion within myself. My clear-minded Priestess Self, collaborated with my passionate womanself to draw that energy inward to create greater fusion between my masculine and feminine aspects of Self. I have relaxed into an eternal embrace. Love I did not know how to give or receive flows freely without expectations or conditions.

Though we would not have used these words twenty-five years ago when we met, I now realize that the woman I am has always seen the God in him, and the man he is has always seen the Goddess in me. Caressed by this knowing, I feel no longing for what was or might have been between us. But I do feel an awakening, a remembering of the Sacred Union of a Soul that divided in half, one part masculine, the other feminine, in order to experience individuated life. I no longer need *incentive* to create space for a partner. I need only feel my soul longing for itself, to feel the God and Goddess Within yearning to become the One. I need to completely *trust the process.*

᪥

And so it came to pass. The mysteries in the temple scrolls that I carried have been revealed. The teaching has been brought forth that we are, each and every one of us, Priest and Priestess to the World. Earth is again the temple. Sky, its expansive ceiling. The people are awakening to the knowing that they need no outside intermediaries between Heaven and Earth. This knowing activates memory of our own Divinity as Sons and Daughters of our Mother Goddess/Father God. And as we mature in consciousness, we walk the Sacred Earth as Gods and Goddesses, as the new Archetypes of the New Earth in the ever unfolding, co-created sacred story of Creation. We know the Great Mystery in the only way it can be known . . . BY LIVING IT, BY BEING IT!

Appendixes

The Priestess Archetype
by Nicole Christine

This article was written for my monthly "Dancing the Circle" relationship column in the November 1994 issue of The Awareness Journal. I am most grateful to Publisher Pam Rierson and her staff for their unwavering commitment to the spiritual awakening of humanity and the Planet. And many thanks go to Dennis Meade-Shikaly, who writes a male perspective to each monthly topic, for his dedication to the healing process between women and men.

Awakening the Priestess Aspect in women is the primary focus of my inner and outer spiritual work. At this transitional phase of humanity's evolution, this focus is significant in archetypal dimensions as they are expressing today. As we transition out of the patriarchal era, the Goddess and Priestess reemerge to co-create an evolved partnership with God and Priest based on the best of matriarchy and patriarchy. In this context, the Priestess comes alive for me.

During matriarchy, the Priestess and Priest served as intermediaries between the Gods and Goddesses on humanity's behalf. In Jungian terms, this intermediary role is the *medial* archetype. Viewing Creation as energy or vibrational fields and Earth as having a very dense energy field, it is easy to see that humanity literally had its hands full simply surviving. Most people felt unable to tap into the higher vibrational fields of Deity. Seeking mediation, they turned to persons who devoted their lives to tapping into energetically finer vibrations.

For a long period, the Priestess communed with the Goddess of many faces. But she, who called on Artemis, the Goddess of the Forest, for strength on behalf of maidens . . . or Hestia, the Goddess of the Hearth, for nurturing patience for mothers . . . or Hecate, the Goddess of the Crossroads, for wisdom for women of years, faded from view when a consortless God began to rule the lives of much of humanity. In this domain, intercessional powers were attributed to Rabbis, Priests, and Ministers. Women, called to serve the Divine, played supportive roles as nuns or wives to these male mediators.

Now, we are at another crossroads. The power of the multi-denominational Church is diminishing. Gurus are falling from grace. Father God heaven-centered religions are having to move over to make room for the resurgence of Mother Goddess earth-centered traditions. Does this mean a return of the Priestess as a medial archetype for humanity? Does this portend the re-building of Goddess Temples? I think not.

I think we have evolved our capacity to energetically merge heaven and earth on our own behalf. I believe enough of us have lifted our sights beyond sheer survival to see the sacredness in all life. I sense that fewer of us are looking to external representatives of the Divine. We are awakening to the Universal Mother/Father within us. And if the Goddess and God are within, so, too, are the Priestess and the Priest. Thus we become conscious of our bodies, our homes, our workplaces as temples. We realize that our very Earth is a Living Temple. We take down our religious walls of separation and honor everyone's Earth-walk as sacred. We align the vibrational fields of our human/worldly selves with our Priest-ess/sacred selves and with our God-dess/Divine Selves.

In my work to Awaken the Priestess, I am enthralled to witness each woman soften into the sacred feminine and radiantly bring forth amazing strength activated for the Highest Good. She becomes a Priest-ess to the World. The woman she is walks in harmony with all creatures. The Priestess she is knows all life as Sacred. The Goddess she is sees and honors the God/Goddess in everyone.

Through the Priestess Awakening Process, she re-births the maiden. She is, once again, virginal

—sovereign and whole unto herself. She consciously makes choices that nurture and honor her authentic self and the authentic selves of others.

Then comes a redefinition of her mother aspect. She experiences her oneness with our Earth Mother and our Universal Mother. She examines her need to mother by giving and nurturing that which she births. She acknowledges her need to be mothered by receiving and being nurtured.

Now she **reclaims** her Priestess self. She internalizes and integrates her outer-directed, worldly experiences by calling them into the center of her being. Then she rests. From this place of stillness, she is able to sanctify all her experiences. She quietly and gratefully listens to her Sacred Self. She remembers there is no good and bad, no right and wrong. Life simply IS. She regains cosmic perspective and mediates between the consciousness of her woman self and her Goddess Self.

This progression prepares her for Cronehood. Now she is ready to bring forth the wisdom of long life to those in the world who choose to hear. As Crone, she **reunites** all archetypes as needed, then transcends them. Transcending even the crone archetype.

With the re-emergence of the sacred feminine, attention is, again, being given to the archetypal Moon Goddess Aspects. The waxing moon corresponds to the maiden, the full moon to the mother, and the dark moon to the crone. Slowly, there is a reinstating of the waning aspect. For some, this is the queen or the matriarch. For others, it is the Priestess.

These aspects or archetypes are available to us whatever our age or phase. The Priestess helps the maiden prepare for her sacred journey. The mother reminds the Priestess that she, too, needs personal attention. The crone wisely aids the mother in guiding her children. The maiden is alive in the crone whose tired bones still dance.

My Sacred Work/Play to Awaken the Priestess is a celebration of these four aspects of the Moon Goddess. Through this process, I am able to hold the space for woman's greatness, for humanity's greatness. By tapping into the archetypal energies of the Priestess, I see our Divinity and the Sacredness of All Life. It is my prayer that all people awaken to their own capacity for *inner-mediation* and consistently experience and radiate their direct connection to their Higher Source. So be it.

Nicole Christine expresses as a writer, process facilitator, and spiritual mentor. She is an ordained Priestess of Gaia in the International Fellowship of Isis and an Initiate of Mary in the Madonna Ministries. She can be reached through:

Earth Song Publications
3400 E. Speedway, Suite 118-288
Tucson, AZ 85716.

Photo by Scott Weisman.

Temple of the Living Earth & The Fellowship of Isis

The Seeding, The Sprouting

This circular explains the corresponding relationship between the International Fellowship of Isis, the Temple of the Living Earth, and the Awakening the Priestess Process. The matrix for the *Awakening Process* was formed via my doctoral discourse, *The Temple of Gaia & Green Man,* in early 1992. I did the Goddess inspired doctoral work as a Priestess of Gaia ordained in the Fellowship of Isis (FOI). It contained the Divine Design for activating Priest/Priestess of the World and Temple of the Living Earth (TLE) consciousness.

This Sacred Work was seeded that spring when I established Earth Song Institute, Temple and Shop in Tucson, Arizona. The soil was tilled. Seeds were sown and nurtured. At the end of that year, I was guided to sell the business of *gardening* to another. I traveled for most of 1993, reflecting and resting from the labors of the year before. I was tired and not conscious that my work was going through a gestation period.

Back in Tucson, early in 1994, it suddenly sprouted as a circle of Priestess Initiates committed to awakening the Inner Priestess. This formation was a collaborative effort between the new Temple *gardener* and me. Growth was rapid! By March 1995, four circles (one in Northern Arizona) organically emerged into a Priestess Sisterhood of forty-four amazing women. December 1995, the fourth circle ordination established the final foundational cornerstone of our Sacred Work. Ways are being explored to respond to interest expressed by women in other states and countries and to involve children, young people, and men while sustaining a bonded Sisterhood.

Fellowship of Isis

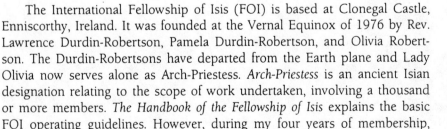

The International Fellowship of Isis (FOI) is based at Clonegal Castle, Enniscorthy, Ireland. It was founded at the Vernal Equinox of 1976 by Rev. Lawrence Durdin-Robertson, Pamela Durdin-Robertson, and Olivia Robertson. The Durdin-Robertsons have departed from the Earth plane and Lady Olivia now serves alone as Arch-Priestess. *Arch-Priestess* is an ancient Isian designation relating to the scope of work undertaken, involving a thousand or more members. *The Handbook of the Fellowship of Isis* explains the basic FOI operating guidelines. However, during my four years of membership, my experience is that Lady Olivia's work is well established on the Inner Realms and she operates on the basis of Divine Inspiration and Guidance.

The Priestly line comes to the Robertsons through hereditary connection to the Egyptian Princess Scota, hereditary Daughter of Isis. It is through this family Priesthood that ordination is bestowed through the ceremony "Ordination of Priestesses and Priests." FOI Priesthood involves acceptance of special work undertaken for the Divine Plan of a particular Goddess, or Goddess and God.

I was ordained in the Madonna Ministry, August 16, 1986, in Ojai, California and began inner work as an Initiate of the Mary. This training in holding the vision or Immaculate Concept of a spiritual destiny prepared me for the work to come. Training in the former FOI College of Isis in Tucson, led to my ordination as a Priestess of Gaia at Summer Solstice, June 21, 1991. On March 16, 1992, I was enrolled as a Doctor of Divinity in the Fellowship. On April 23, I was acknowledged as Priestess Hierophant, D.D., chartered founder of the "Lyceum of Gaia: Earth Song" through the Collegium Isidis. *Heirophant* simply means *guide* and indicates that one has taken on greater responsibility than was the case as a Priestess or Priest. On May 5, 1994, I was certified as founder of The Iseum of Gaia & the Green Man. The Iseum has since been renamed as the Iseum of Inner Wisdom. My affiliation between FOI and my work of facilitating/guiding the *Awakening the Priestess Process* is via my Iseum status.

One needs to be a member of FOI in order to be ordained. The Ordination Rite must be performed by an FOI Priest or Priestess. I perceive FOI as a primary global channel for the re-emergence of the Goddess in harmony with the God and membership, therein, as an energetic alignment with this accelerating momentum. FOI respects the freedom of conscience of each member. There are no vows required and no commitments to secrecy. All Fellowship activities are optional and members are free to resign or rejoin at their own choice. Membership is free. Each member has the option of taking out a paid subscription to the *Isian News* quarterly newsletter. Members range from individuals on solitary paths in remote areas to persons of considerable renown. Numbers are approaching 13,000 in 80 countries.

Lyceums and Iseums are for FOI members only. College of Isis Lyceums offer a structured Magi Degree Course in FOI Liturgy. I took inactive Lyceum status when I sold Earth Song. One must be ordained to found a Lyceum. In February 1995, there were 58 Lyceums in 12 countries and 57 Hierophants.

An Iseum is a *Hearth of the Goddess*. When one is inspired by the Goddess to found an Iseum, the Clonegal Castle Foundation Iseum is notified and, when it is accepted, a Charter is issued. Iseums function autonomously. Unlike Lyceums that offer FOI Liturgy, Iseum founders have the right to determine their own course. There are no binding oaths in any Iseum and members may practice any other path or religion in conjunction and may leave freely at any time. Each individual Iseum is a focus for work and the workers must be in harmony. Iseum circles are viewed as spirals reaching out to the cosmos. Physical space may be a member's home, a sacred site, or a more public place. As of February 1995, there were 451 Iseums in 37 countries and 441 Priests and Priestesses in 22 countries.

One may communicate with Lady Olivia Robertson by writing to her at Clonegal Castle, Enniscorthy, Ireland. Order forms for FOI materials and a listing of Lyceums and Iseums are available.

Temple Of The Living Earth

Herein lies the heart and soul of my Sacred Work. My dedication in this lifetime as a Priestess, a human being, and a citizen of the Universe is to Gaia, Earth Goddess, and to her/our process of rising up into higher consciousness of symbiotic union between Heaven and Earth, spirit and matter, masculine and feminine, inner and outer. The *Temple of the Living Earth* is a thoughtform. In other words, it is a concept held in consciousness that the Earth is a sacred, living entity with a destiny of her own. This destiny includes allowing humanity to inhabit her body in order for humanity to fulfill its destiny. I believe that humanity's Highest Destiny is to co-create with Earth in a Sacred Way that brings forth and sustains harmony, beauty and balance.

I used to have grandiose notions about saving the World by changing the political, economic, and social systems. Now I work with what I experience as basics. To honor the body of our Earth Mother as a Temple. To honor my own body as a Temple. To relate to my home as sacred space and be in conscious relationship with all I own. To reclaim the hearth of homes as spiritual centers where the warmth and guidance of woman are a family's, a community's, source of inspiration. To inspire interaction with, reverence for, and celebration of nature.

To the degree that I live these basics . . . to the degree I make my Earthwalk sacred . . . to the degree I embody and energize the thoughtform of the Temple of the Living Earth . . . to these degrees, I am a Priestess to the World.

The Temple of the Living Earth (TLE) is not an organization. There is no membership, free or otherwise. It is the act of consciously, lovingly, embracing Life on Earth in body, mind, heart, and soul. The *Awakening the Priestess Process* was revealed to me as a way of activating and energizing the Temple of the Living Earth thoughtform by helping to re-awaken the Priests and Priestesses to the World.

The Iseum of Inner Wisdom (formerly the Iseum of Gaia and the Green Man) utilizes the Earth Song Publications address. For me, the Iseum is a working principle, rather than a place. Within the FOI structure, Initiates working with me are members of this Iseum and thus eligible for ordination through the Fellowship. As an FOI Priestess, I joyfully do my part to prepare and consecrate the Initiates who are desirous of being ordained in the Fellowship of Isis in co-creative alignment with whatever aspect of the Goddess that they chose.

Within the TLE construct, as Initiates, we are Sacred Sisters to one another and Divine Daughters of our Earth Mother. *Membership* is a matter of the heart. *Eligibility* for ordination as a Priestess to the World, a Priestess of Gaia, arises from a deep inner knowing that we share a co-creative destiny with this Earth Goddess Rising. As a Crystal Priestess of Gaia, I wholeheartedly support those choosing to remember this destiny and will, when feasible, ceremonially stand witness to my sisters' self-proclaimed awakening as Priestesses to the World. As an Initiate of Mary, I uphold the Immaculate Concept of the Awakening of the Priestess in every woman. As a proponent of a freely evolving, ever expanding Priestess Sisterhood, I support you in making a choice to independently design and activate your own process.

It is my delight and honor to share in the reclaiming of our Sacred Selves and Sisterhood as Priestesses.

Nicole Christine,
Crystal Priestess of Gaia
Earth Song Publications
3400 E. Speedway Blvd. Suite 118-288
Tucson, AZ 85716

Temple Of The Living Earth

The Earth is a Living Spiritual Being in Her Own Right, with Her Own mind, consciousness, destiny and development. The Earth, Gaia, is a living organism within the Universal Living Organism. She is a Sacred Site. She is our Church, Temple, Sanctuary, Home, and Mother.

Guiding Principles Of Earth/Gaian-Centered Spirituality

Honor Earth/Gaia as a Sacred site and partake of her Fruit joyfully and gratefully. Honor the Life Force in ALL. Honor your body, hearth, and workplace as Temples of the Divine.

Live every moment as a Sacred Act in Alignment with Divine Source as you know and experience It.

Know Self as a unique, actualized, multi-dimensional, regenerative Being of unlimited creative and loving potential within the Cosmic Whole.

Live open-mindedly, thinking and feeling independently, for the Greatest Good. Unlearn false and outmoded teachings and conditionings. Gratefully exercise the gift of the right of free will, responsibly and honestly.

Live in Freedom by breaking through form into formless form into Spirit and Wholeness.

Know the Silence and merge with It. Honor the creative power of the Word. Avoid unnecessary, unclear verbiage and waste of the priceless Breath of Life.

Live and speak the Highest Truth, as you know it, moment-to-moment, for the Highest Good. Honor and encourage the Highest Truth of others in the darkness and the light.

Stimulate inner awareness and multi-sensory perceptions to heighten communication with ALL LIFE and enhance Cosmic consciousness. Commune with Father Sky and Mother Earth as directly and respectfully as a Loving Child communes with Loving Parents.

Commit to the Sacred Marriage through inner union of the Divine Feminine and Divine Masculine, of feeling and thought.

Live responsibly in co-creative, co-operative partnership with the Earth, Nature and One Another.

Live in Balance, Beauty, Love, Harmony and Good Humor.

Live attentively. Trust, attune and respond to the synchronistic Life Process.

Live in the natural flow of Abundance, Simplicity and All Good Things. Give and receive generously.

LIVE LIFE FULLY AND GRATEFULLY!
CELEBRATE CREATION!

Manifesto

Growing numbers of people are rediscovering their love for the Goddess. At first, this love may seem to be no more than an inner feeling. But soon it develops: it becomes a longing to help the Goddess actively in the manifestation of Her divine plan. Thus, one hears such inquiries as, "How can I get Initiated into the Mysteries of the Goddess? How can I experience a closer communion with her? Where are her nearest temples and devotees? How can I join the Priesthood of the Goddess?" and many other such questions.

The Fellowship of Isis has been founded to answer these needs. Membership provides means of promoting a closer communion between the Goddess and each member, both singly and as part of a larger group. There are hundreds of Iseums and thousands of members all over the World, since the Fellowship was founded in 1976 by Lawrence, Pamela and Olivia Durdin-Robertson. Love, Beauty, and Truth are expressed through a multi-religious, multi-cultural, multi-racial Fellowship. The good in all faiths is honored. Membership is free.

The Fellowship is organized on a democratic basis. All members have equal privileges within it, whether as a single member or part of an Iseum or Lyceum. This manifesto applies also to the daughter societies: the College of Isis, the Order of Tara, and the Druid Clan of Dana.

The Fellowship respects the freedom of conscience of each member. There are no vows required or commitments to secrecy. All Fellowship activities are optional and members are free to resign or rejoin at their own choice.

The Fellowship reverences all manifestations of Life. The God also is venerated. The Rites exclude any form of sacrifice, whether actual or symbolic. Nature is revered and conserved. The work of the Order of Tara is for conservation of Nature.

The Fellowship accepts religious toleration and is not exclusivist. Members are free to maintain other religious allegiances. Membership is open to all of every religion, tradition and race. Children, listed as "Children of Isis, are welcomed, subject to parental consent. "The Animal Family of Isis" is listed in every Isian News.

The Fellowship believes in the promotion of Love, Beauty and Abundance. No encouragement is given to asceticism. The Fellowship seeks to develop psychic gifts, happiness, and compassion for all life. The Druid Clan of Dana develops Nature's psychic gifts.

The College of Isis has been revived after its suppression 1,500 years ago. Like Aset Shemsu, the F.O.I. itself, has always been alive in the Inner Planes. It is from these Inner Planes that its return has been inspired. Magi degrees may be conferred through Lyceums of the College. Correspondent courses are offered. There are no vows nor secrecy.

Iseums are the very Hearths of the Goddess and God to Whom they are dedicated. These are listed, along with Lyceums and new members, in every issue of Isian News. Lyceums and Iseums are for F.O.I. members only. Tara Priories and Dana Groves are also listed regularly in Isian News. All these centres are for F.O.I. members only.

The Fellowship of Isis Priesthood is derived from an hereditary line of the Robertsons from Ancient Egypt. Priestesses, Priests, every member, have equal honour. Priestesses and Priests work with the Goddess — or Goddess and God — of their own Faith. Every human, animal, bird, tree is an eternal offspring of the Mother Goddess's Divine Family of Life.

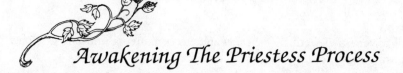

Awakening The Priestess Process

In order to fully re-establish Goddess consciousness in the world and to heighten awareness of our shared journey with our Rising Earth Goddess, Gaia, much of the Sacred Work is currently focused on the Sacred Feminine. The inevitable progression is to bring the evolved Sacred Feminine and Sacred Masculine into harmony and balance. The Divine Design of the Temple of the Living Earth (TLE) incorporates the Sacred Union of the God/Goddess and a Celebratory Community of Priests and Priestesses to the World who mirror the God/Goddess within each of us. The Awakening Process brings the Divine Design to consciousness. Affiliation with the Fellowship of Isis (FOI) establishes linkages to the ancient ways of the Goddess and to international celebrants of the re-emerging Goddess. This Awakening the Priestess Process is unique to the Inner Wisdom Iseum formed by Nicole Christine as a FOI Priestess.

Process Design

The form-alized process covers a period of preparation for initiation and nine months of initiation work in preparation for ordination as a Priestess. It is designed for a circle of 8-12 women and an ordained Priestess facilitator committed to the entire process. Coming together in sacred, nurturing space activates the awakening and remembering. The circle meets twice a month and each Initiate has a monthly private session with the facilitator to personalize the process. The design structure is intended to be gentle and flexible to allow it to take on a life of its own and reflect the evolutionary flow of the daily life of each Initiate. All activities are designed to nurture and support participants and are openly explained. Cost factors are based on equitable exchanges for expenses and energy expenditures of time and talents.

One's Priestess Self is the vibratory intermediary between her womanself and her Goddess Self. Accordingly, each Priestess Initiate will determine her readiness for ordination based on her own Inner Counsel. The shift into the Priestess vibration that takes place during the Ordination Rite is energetically integrated over a period of one year and one day following ordination. Celebratory recognition of the completion of this integration period is recommended.

Process Intention

To awaken the Initiate's Priestess Self that she might bring forth her unique gifts in a sacred way and move into co-creative expression with the Goddess in accordance with her Remembrance and Activation of the Divine Design. To deepen the richness of the Initiate's Inner Life and stimulate her sense of aliveness. To enhance her awareness of patterns and energy flows that she might consciously engage Life Force Energy.

Pre-Initiation – Guidelines for Initiates

1. Meet once with other Initiate Candidates
2. Read Temple of the Living Earth which provides an extensive perspective of the Awakening Process
3. Prepare your Awakening the Priestess Intention Statement indicating your highest intent for the nine month initiation period. Keep it clear and simple. The Universe will handle the details. Create an artistic copy for the altar. This will be returned to you at the time of your ordination. Keep a copy for yourself and give one to the Process Facilitator Priestess 48 hours prior to the ceremony that she may meditate on it in advance.
4. Begin a written telling of your spiritual journey up to the present for purposes of self-reflection and sharing in your circle.

Rite of Initiation

This is a ceremonial ritual to Awaken the Inner Priestess in the Name of the Goddess by activating the vibrational field of the Priestess Initiate. The facilitating Priestess and each Initiate orally presents their written Intentions. Only Initiates and ordained Priestesses are present. To be an Initiate is to be a candidate for an entirely new *DIRECT EXPERIENCE* of spiritual significance. An initiation is the focusing of energy in a pattern that serves evolutionary processes. This Rite of Initiation is performed through the power of each Initiate's own Inner Authority and Divinity.

This ceremonial rite begins with a procession to the entrance of the ceremonial space. There the facilitating Priestess asks each candidate, "Are you fully aware that to participate in this Rite, is to activate the awakening of your Priestess Self?" Receiving an affirmative response, the facilitator then asks the candidate if she is ready to enter. If she is ready, she is smudged with sage or blessed with water by another Priestess.

A third Priestess greets her within the ceremonial space and guides her to a place in the circle. When everyone is present, the ceremony begins with grateful acknowledgment of the Four Directions, the Spirit of Place, and the etheric Beings that are present. The facilitating Priestess then steps to the altar and reads her Intention Statement, which indicates her willing commitment to hold the Immaculate Concept of the Awakening of each Priestess. She places it on the altar and lights a candle. Then she stands ready to hold sacred space for each Initiate as she performs this same ritual act and returns to her space in the circle. It tends to be a very moving experience for all as each woman voices her intent to awaken.

Next, ordained Priestesses offer the Priestess Initiates gifts from the Goddess. Water that she may never thirst. Honey that she may know the sweetness of life. Bread that she may never hunger. And a crystal for clarity in her awakening.

The facilitating Priestess then moves to the center of the circle and aligns the group energies with the energies of the Priestess Oversoul. The Four Directions and the Visible and Invisible Ones are thanked. And the ceremony is ended.

Initiate Process

A Priestess interfaces with Life at the non-judgmental level of patterns and energy flows rather than the judgmental level of personalities and issues. To facilitate mastery of patterns and energy flows, completion of four (4) sessions of Essence Repatterning is highly recommended and reading of *The Celestine Prophecy* and *I Remember Union*. This can be begun prior to initiation or any time during the nine month initiation period, preferably in the first trimester. Other training, such as Reiki and Bio-Magnetics, is valuable. It is recommended that each candidate keep a journal and/or portfolio file of her process. There will be many opportunities to participate in activities with the larger spiritual community.

First Trimester
Focus: KNOW THYSELF

The emphasis is on Self-Knowing and Self-Honoring. This involves: embracing the Stillness where Oneness resides, developing inner directedness, listening intently and open-heartedly, and speaking and living one's truth. This is done in the context of personal discovery of the Ways of the Goddess. Each woman writes the story of her Sacred Journey and shares twenty minutes of it at a Circle meeting. She is honored in a Foot Washing Ritual and receives small altar gifts from her Circle Sisters. The honoring of three women in three hours is a collectively empowering experience. Each Initiate:

1. Meets privately, a minimum of two hours a month, with the facilitating Priestess to focus and give voice to her process
2. Meets twice a month with her Circle of Initiates

Second Trimester
Focus: KNOWING SELF THROUGH NATURE

Woman knows herself best alone, in nature. There she can sort herself out from her relationship-centered existence and nurture her relationship to her Essence Self. Private and Circle meetings focus on experiences, such as Earth-honoring rituals, to heighten this awareness.

1. Private sessions take place in nature at sites chosen by the Initiate
2. One monthly group meeting is held indoors to further group interaction
3. The second monthly group meeting is an outdoor ritual co-created and facilitated by 3-4 Initiates

Third Trimester
Focus: CO-CREATIVE RITUAL & CEREMONY

Initiates explore the significance of ritual and ceremony in daily life. They co-create rituals and ceremonies rising out of personal experience and character in forms that speak to our times, our ways, and link us to our ancient past. The Circle co-creates a Menarche Ritual, a Rite of Rebirth and the Priestess Ordination Rite.

1. Continue private sessions
2. The Menarche and Rebirth rituals take place during the twice monthly group sessions. Small group co-creation of rituals require additional planning time.
3. Prepare for Ordination Ceremony
4. Those choosing to be ordained in the Fellowship of Isis need to write a letter of introduction to Arch-Priestess Lady Olivia Robertson prior to ordination. The letter includes an evaluation of the initiation process. The ordaining Iseum Priestess will send it along with a cover letter verifying ordination. Each Priestess will then receive an ordination certificate from FOI.
5. Those choosing self-proclamation as a Priestess to the World only, are asked to write a short summation and evaluation of their Awakening Process. This is given to the facilitating Priestess prior to the ceremony.

General Ceremonial or Ritual Considerations

Ceremony is a bridge between the reality of the soul and the physical reality. The potency (immediate and long term, personal and universal) of any ritual or ceremony is proportional to the participants' sustained, focused consciousness and intent preceding, during and after the activity. In the last trimester, the synergy of the Ordination Ceremony is energized through individual and collective emotional, mental, physical, and spiritual attention and intention. It is time to be in consistent communication with one's Priestess Self so that the co-created ceremony is a true celebration of her awakening and re-emergence. The primary consideration regarding the co-created ceremony is that a resonating cord is struck between participants and that all the components are personally significant and relevant to participants

The essence of a ceremony has four key aspects: 1) energetic attunement with place, purpose, physical and etheric participants, 2) personal relevance, 3) co-creative synergy, 4) focused celebratory attention. (Even grieving ceremonies are celebratory in the sense of engaging Life on Life's terms.)

The components and intent of a ritual or ceremony, from a Hopi perspective, are 1) form/rules, 2) symbols/objects/place, 3) song/performance/words, 4) dance/rhythm. The intent is to excite emotions and a sense of aesthetics and to bring forth power for good for all clans. The ritual or ceremony has universality — hope for life through faith, industry, cooperation, and love.

Fellowship of Isis Ordination

Components according to the Ordination of Priestesses and Priests by Olivia Robertson:

1. The Scribe reads out the Initiate's degrees, appointments and achievements
2. The Initiate offers all this in divine service and presents tokens of dedication on the altar
3. The ordaining Priest-ess accepts these offerings in the name of the Goddess and bestows Divine blessings on the Initiate
4. The Initiate declares the name of the Goddess whose path she is choosing to follow
5. The ordination is performed through the ordaining Priest-ess anointing the candidate with oil in the name of the chosen Goddess (this is the key requirement)
6. The New Priestess is then crowned and receives her stole and wand that she made (these represent true vision, the heart of love, and the will to use creative power for good)
7. The Rite is witnessed by Priestesses and Priests who declare that they accept the New Priestess to their ranks
8. The ordaining Priest-ess declares the new Priestess to be daughter of the Goddess with conscious enjoyment of day and night, summer and winter, sun and moon. She is whole.

The intent is that the Initiate dedicates her life, however she sees fit to live it, to Divine Purpose. The Priestess of today and tomorrow has the equivocal advantage of past suppression. She has learned charity and endurance. For only those who know how best to serve can rule well. A Priestess does not rule men, nor races. She rules the striving elements of her own being, and through understanding the law of transmutation, creates harmony of mind, heart and body. Thus, she may teach others that which she can do herself.

Temple of the Living Earth Proclamation Ceremony

From the Temple of the Living Earth perspective, the ordination ceremony is one of self-proclamation by the Initiate as a Priestess to the World. The components and intent reflect the calling identified by the Initiate. To self-proclaim one's self as a Priestess to the World is to live, move, and experience Being-ness in the high vibrational energy field of this Celestial Earth archetype . . . it is to dance with the New Earth archetypes revealed through the *Gaia Matrix Oracle*. As a Priestess of Gaia, you embrace your role in the Divine Design of Earth, Nature, and humanity's ascension into higher consciousness bringing about the marriage of Heaven and Earth, spirit and matter, within and without, mind and body, thought and feeling, masculine and feminine.

In the ancient ways of the Goddess, a Priestess chose to serve the Divine Feminine Principle in one of two ways: 1) to do service to the Goddess you were dedicated to when She asked it of you, or 2) devote your life to serving Her. In the evolving ways of the Goddess, a Priestess to the World commits to co-creating a New Earth Fulfilled with Gaia, other self-aligned Gods and Goddesses, and the New Earth Archetypes. In so doing, the New Priestess commits, according to her own Guidance, to honor the Great Goddess by honoring herself, to uphold the thoughtform of the Temple of the Living Earth, and to evolve into Goddess-Realized consciousness. This frees her from Warrior consciousness and the belief in/battle against *good and evil* and moves her through Healer consciousness into the consciousness of Co-Creators and Celebrants of Life.

The following declaration may be made by a witnessing Priestess to the World to acknowledge her proclamation. *You, _____, are Celestial Earth. Your body is illumined. You are one with Heaven and Earth. Give freely of your True Self for the Greatest Good of All. And in a pure act of devotion, as Virgins of Virgins, co-creatively construct a New World Fulfilled in Harmony and Beauty. It is done and it is so and All Creation gives thanks.*

Following the ceremony, you may sign your name to a Temple of the Living Earth certificate to anchor your proclamation. Space is provided for a witnessing signature.

Fellowship of Isis & Priestess to the World Ordination

To choose ordination in FOI and as a Priestess to the World is to honor the Goddess Isis Lineage that birthed the New Priestess of the Temple of the Living Earth. It is to choose to be a bridge between the Old and the New in this decade of great transformation. It is to Heal and to Co-Create/Celebrate. It is to seed the New Reality while keeping the path clear that others may find their way from the Old Reality bringing only that which truly serves the New with them. It is to model how to cross the abyss of reactivity that separates the Worlds by responsibly embracing Life. The ceremonial design reflects this intention and integrates the components of the individual FOI and TLE ceremonies.

Rite Of Ordination

Initiates step forth in ceremony as Priestesses ready to carry that vibration in the World. Each Initiate determines her readiness and intention based on her inner knowing and communion with the Goddess. The newly consecrated Priestesses are embraced by the Goddess and welcomed into the community of Priestesses. Guests may be present.

ORDINATION INTENT: To ceremonially open to be permeated by the Priestess vibration in conscious alignment with the Goddess aspects the candidate is embracing and being embraced by —knowing that the year and a day to follow will be a sacred period in which she becomes the embodiment of these Divine Qualities.

ORDINATION CHOICES: 1) ordained as a Priestess in the Fellowship of Isis (FOI) aligned with the Goddess(es) with whom you identify, 2) ordained by self-proclamation as a Priestess to the World/Priestess of Gaia (and any other Goddesses), 3) ordained in both choices.

INTERPRETATION OF CHOICES:
1. To be ordained in FOI is to call forth the ancient ways of the Goddess fitting for these times and to align with this international vehicle/channel for the reemerging Goddess.
2. To be a self-proclaimed Priestess to the World is to profess one's intent to uphold the Thoughtform of the Temple of the Living Earth and to consciously participate in Gaia's transformation into Celestial Earth where Heaven and Earth, spirit and matter, masculine and feminine unite.
3. To chose both is to integrate the Old with the New, thus completing with the Old to bring forth *the best of what has been* as an affirming foundation for the New.

Legal Factors

As a Fellowship of Isis Priestess, one may establish a FOI Temple, Lyceum or Iseum and use the title "The Reverend." FOI is not involved with governmental legalities. Legal status to perform legally binding ceremonies can only be gained state by state, country by country. Options tend to be either obtaining religious non-profit status or a business license as a self-employed minister operating under the licensing category deemed appropriate by the licensing agency. Tax regulations apply at the Federal, State, County and City levels. It is important to become informed of legal requirements in the jurisdiction where one chooses to *minister*.

A Priestess to the World consciously aligns with Cosmic Laws. She does not enmesh herself in the laws of the Patriarchs or energize these passing ways through hostile opposition. We journeyed through the tunnel from the Temple of the Mother where feminine power was worshipped into the Kingdom where the Father Principle of worshipping male power reigned. Now we are moving through yet another tunnel to a New Earth where the Mother/Father Principle is upheld and the God/Goddess within us reigns. Thus we are called upon to co-create new ceremonies, rituals, and guidelines for living that reflect this evolution in consciousness and the Remembrance of Union. We have traveled long and well! It is time to come into our Fullness.

SEAL One Year and One Day

The cellular and energetic integration of the internalized Priestess vibration is complete one year and one day after ordination. Celebratory acknowledgment of this completion is a joy to the Soul of the Awakened Priestess!

Nicole Christine
Earth Song Publications
3400 Speedway Blvd. Suite 118-288 • Tucson, AZ 85716

Bibliography/Recommended Reading List

I have a small, intimate collection of books. My relationship to them is as varied as my relationships to people. Some are messengers. Others are validators or challengers. Some are simply good friends. There are books I read cover-to-cover and ones I only scan or read in portions. On occasion, a single line speaks to me and I know all I need to know from that book. At times, I feel the essence of the writing without even reading the book. Yet each book, in its own way, has contributed much to my personal development and the development of this book. Such is my varied degree of familiarity with the books listed here.

Infinite gratitude goes to the owners and personnel of Tucson's fine spiritually oriented bookstores. You have done much to enhance my life. Thank you Antigone's; Avalon, the Inner Isle; Awakenings; the Book Mark; the Light House; Peace of Mind; and Rainbow Moods!

Allen, Paula Gunn. *The Sacred Hoop*. Boston: Beacon Press, 1986.

Anderson, Wm. *GREEN MAN - The Archetype of our Oneness with the Earth*. NY: HarperCollins, 1990.

Austin, Hallie Oglehart. *Heart Of The Goddess*. Berkeley: Wingbow Press, 1990.

Belanger, J.D. *The Place Called Attar*. Waterloo, WI: Countryside Publications, Ltd., 1990. (W8333 Doepke Rd. Waterloo, WI 53594)

Bonnell, Gary. *ASCENSION - The Original Teachings of Christ Awareness*. Denver, CO: Richman Rose Pub. 1991.

Bradley, Marion Zimmer. *The Firebrand*. NY: Pocket Books, 1988.

Bradley, Marion Zimmer. *Forest House*. NY: Penguin Books, 1993.

Bradley, Marion Zimmer, *Mists Of Avalon*. NY: Ballantine, 1982.

Bridges, Carol. *The Medicine Woman Inner Guidebook & Tarot Deck*. Stanford, CT: U.S. Games Systems, Inc., 1991.

Brooke Medicine Eagle. *Buffalo Woman Comes Singing*. NY: Ballantine, 1991.

Calhoun, Flo. *I Remember Union*. Bethlehem, CT: All Worlds Pub., 1992.

Christine, Nicole. *My Ascension Journal*. Livermore, CA: Oughten House Pub., 1995.

Clow, Barbara Hand. *Heart Of The Christos*. Santa Fe, NM: Bear & Co., 1991

Clow, Barbara Hand. *Liquid Light Of Sex*. Santa Fe, NM: Bear & Co., 1991.

Cott, Jonathan. *Isis and Osiris*. NY: Doubleday, 1994.

Duerk, Judith. *Circle Of Stones*. San Diego, CA: LuraMedia, 1990.

Duerk, Judith. *I Sit Listening To The Wind*. San Diego, CA: LuraMedia, 1990.

Eisler, Riane. *The Chalice and the Blade*. SF: Harper, 1988.

Erbe, Peter. *God I Am*. Australia: Triad Pub., 1991.

Giamario, Daniel & Brent, Carolyn. *The Shamanic Astrology Handbook*. Tucson, AZ: J.C. Assoc. Unltd., 1995. (P.O. Box 35325, Tucson, AZ 85740)

Griscom, Chris. *Ageless Body*. Galisteo, NM: Light Institute Press, 1992.

Griscom, Chris. *Feminine Fusion*. NY: Simon & Schuster, 1991.

Griscom, Chris. *The Healing of Emotion – Awakening the Fearless Self*. NY: Simon & Schuster, 1988

Hay, Louise. *Love Your Body*. Carson, CA: Hay House, 1989.

Johnson, Kenneth & Elsbeth, Marguerite. *The Grail Castle*. St. Paul, MN: Llewellyn Pub., 1995.

Johnson, Kenneth & Elsbeth, Marguerite. *The Silver Wheel*. St. Paul, MN: Llewellyn Pub., 1995.

Judith Laura. *SHE LIVES! The Return of Our Great Mother*. Freedom, CA 95019: The Crossing Press, 1989.

Kemp, Cynthia. *Flower Essences: Bridges to the Soul*. Tucson, AZ: Desert Alchemy, 1988. (P.O. Box 44189, Tucson, AZ 85733)

King, Jani. *An Act of Faith – The P'Taah Tapes*. Australia: Triad Pub., 1991.

Kinstler, Clysta. *The Moon Under Her Feet*. SF: Harper, 1985.

Klien, Eric. *THE CRYSTAL STAIR – A Guide to Ascension*. Livermore, CA: Oughten House Pub., 1992.

Kryder, Rowena Pattee. *GAIA MATRIX ORACLE Vol I: Worlds, Major Arcana & Symbols*. Mt. Shasta, CA: Golden Point Productions, 1990. (P.O. Box 940, Mt. Shasta, CA 96067)

Kryder, Rowena Pattee. *GAIA MATRIX ORACLE Vol II: Readings for Worlds, Major Arcana & Symbols*. Mt. Shasta, CA: Golden Point Productions, 1990.

Kryder, Rowena Pattee. *Sacred Ground to Sacred Space*. Santa Fe, NM: Bear & Co., 1994.

Llywelyn, Morgan. *The Horse Goddess*. NY: Pocket Books, 1983.

Marciniak, Barbara. *Bringers of the Dawn*. Santa Fe, NM: Bear & Co., 1992.

Marciniak, Barbara. *Earth – Pleiadian Keys to the Living Library*. Santa Fe, NM: Bear & Co., 1995.

McCallum, Pat. *Stepping Free of Limiting Patterns with Essence Repatterning*. Chevy Chase, MD: Source Unlimited, 1992.

Michael, Arnold. *Blessed Among Women*. Westlake Village, CA: Gray Pub., 1986.

Ozaniec, Naomi. *Daughters of the Goddess*. London: Aquarian Press, 1993.

Patton, Arnold. *Money and Beyond*. Sylva, NC: Celebration Press, 1993.

Printz, Thomas. *Memoirs of Beloved Mary*. Mt. Shasta, CA: Ascended Master Teaching Fdn. 1986.

Redfield, James. *The Celestine Prophecy*. NY: Warner Books, 1993.

Richardson, Alan. *Earth God Rising – The Return of the Male Mysteries*. St. Paul, MI: Llewellyn Press, 1990.

Robertson, Olivia & Lawrence Durdin. Fellowship of Isis Publications. Cesara Publications, Clonegal Castle, Enniscorthy, Ireland.

Sams, Jamie. *The 13 Original Clan Mothers*. SF: Harper, 1993.

Shepsut, Asia. *Journey of the Priestess*. SF: Aquarian Press, 1993.

Solara. *THE STAR-BORNE: A Remembrance for the Awakened Ones*. Charlottesville, VA: Starborne Ultd., 1989.

Spilsbury, Ariel & Bryner, Michael. *The Mayan Oracle*. Santa Fe, NM: Bear & Co., 1992.

St. Germain through Azena. *Earth's Birth Changes*. Australia: Triad Pub., 1993.

Stewart, R.J. *Celebrating the Male Mysteries*. Great Britain: Arcania Press, 1991.

Stubbs, Tony. *An Ascension Handbook*. Livermore, CA: Oughten House Pub., 1993.

Sun Bear & Wabun. *The Medicine Wheel – Earth Astrology*. Englewood Cliffs, NJ: Prentice-Hall, 1980.

Williamson, Marianne. *A Woman's Worth*. NY: Random House, 1993.

Ywahoo, Dhyani. *Voices of Our Ancestors – Cherokee Teachings from the Wisdom Fire*. Boston: Shambhala, 1987.

Endnotes

The synchronistic way these references wove their way into my experience at such perfect times still amazes me!

1. I wrote this pledge when I began working with the *Gaia Matrix Oracle (GMO)*. I took words directly from the text with some personal adaptations. I have not been able to relocate the pages I referred to then. I include these words with great appreciation for the work of Rowena Pattee Kryder.
2. "A Personal Message From Chris Griscom," a cassette recording; The Light Institute.
3. *GMO Vol. II*, page 192.
4. Adapted from "Spiritual Ecology & the Gaia Matrix" by Rowena Pattee Kryder; March/April 1991, *New Realities Magazine*.
5. The ritual lines are adapted from *GMO Vol. II*, pages 129,133.
6. *GMO Vol. I; Text*, page 26.
7. *Dying Young* by Marti Leimbach; NY: Ivy Books, influenced my decision to determine my own course of relating to my dis-ease. The movie, unfortunately, departed from the book and the dying "hero" relinquished his body and soul to others.
8. The journal entries were influenced by *She Lives!* By Judith Laura, pages 137, 30.
9. For further expansion of "The Directions and Their Attributes," see *Voices Of Our Ancestors* by Dhyani Ywahoo, page 280.
10. Reading by Phoenix Ellaé Elinwood; Del Mar, CA, 1986.
11. See "James Swan On Aligning Oneself With Sacred Places" an interview by Forrest Craver in the April-June 1991 issue of *Wingspan – Journal Of The Male Spirit* (P.O. Box 1941, Manchester, MA 01944).
12. Ibid.
13. *GMO VOL. II*, page 259.
14. *The Star-borne* by Solara, page 125.
15. Ibid, page 127.
16. Ibid, pages 127, 128.
17. Ibid, page 54.
18. Reference inspired by preview clip of the movie *Legends of the Fall*.
19. "Gene of Isis" references inspired by *Earth Birth Changes*, St. Germain through Azena, pages 1 & 2.

Resources

Institutes

Creative Harmonics Institute
Box 940
Mount Shasta, CA 96067

Earth Song/Iseum of Inner Wisdom
3400 E. Speedway, Ste 118-288
Tucson, AZ 85716

The Light Institute
Rt. 3 Box 50
Galisteo, NM 87540

Publications

Awareness Journal (A Monthly Newspaper for Human Potential)
Box 57130
Tucson, AZ 85732-7130

Earth Song Publications
3400 E. Speedway, Ste. 118-288
Tucson, AZ 85716

Golden Point Productions (Rowena Pattee Kryder)
Box 940
Mt. Shasta, CA 96067

J.C. Associates Unlimited (Shamanic Astrology)
Box 91498
Tucson, AZ 85752-1498

Oughten House Publications (Ascension materials)
Box 2008
Livermore, CA 94551-2008

Light Technology Publishing (Sedona Journal of EMERGENCE!)
Box 1526
Sedona, AZ 86339

The World Times (Inspiring news from around the World)
120 Overlook, Rt. 7
Box 124 R
Santa Fe, NM 87505

Shamanic Astrologers

Carolyn Brent
Box 91498
Tucson, AZ 85752-1498

Daniel Giamario
Box 4096
Silver City, NM 88062

Earth Song Publications

Earth Song Publications is a seedling operation dedicated to disseminating Celestial Earth consciousness. If you resonate with this intent and feel guided to contribute to the expansion of this work, your support will be joyfully appreciated. Below are ways such support might take form.

- ❧ *Share the concept of The Temple of the Living Earth.*

- ❧ *Meditate on the written and artistic expressions of the thoughtform of the Temple of the Living Earth. Allow this thoughtform to permeate your consciousness, your life.*

- ❧ *Encourage others to purchase and read copies of the book.*

- ❧ *Give the book as gifts.*

- ❧ *Ask your area bookstores to carry it.*

- ❧ *Financially contribute to Earth Song Publications. Contributions are not tax-deductible. They are, however, an excellent investment in the paradigm shift from Old Earth to New Earth consciousness. Donations will be used to print and distribute more copies of The Temple of the Living Earth.*

Nicole Christine and other Priestesses to the World are available to assist in the activation of the Awakening the Priest-ess Process in your area. For further information, write Nicole at Earth Song Publications.

TEMPLE OF THE LIVING EARTH ORDER INFORMATION

_____ 1 - 9 copies @ $16 each: $_____

_____ 10 or more copies @ $14 each: $_____

Subtotal: $_____

Arizona residents add 7% sales tax: $_____

Shipping & Handling: $__3.00__

Total USA $ (check or money order): $_____

Name _____

Address _____

City _____ State _____ Zip _____

❖

Send payment and make checks payable to:

Earth Song Publications
3400 E. Speedway Blvd.,
Ste. 118-288
Tucson, AZ 85716

❖

_____ Please put me on Earth Song Publications' mailing list. I understand that ESP will not transfer this information to other individuals or businesses.